GOLF SIMPLIFIED

Edward C. Acree and Jock Hutchison

GOLF
Simplified

by

EDWARD C. ACREE
JOCK HUTCHISON
BILL HUTCHISON

ZIFF-DAVIS PUBLISHING COMPANY
CHICAGO • NEW YORK

PREFACE

ONE OF THE reasons why golf is so popular is not only because it is so interesting as a sport, but because it is so healthful. The person who plays not only gets the benefit of the muscle-hardening which comes from the actual swinging of clubs, but gets a few miles of oxygen on the hoof; and about the best place for a person to leave hoofprints is on the hills and dales of the life-giving out-of-doors.

I have listened to golf instructions by the hour and have watched the poor pupils working away and trying with wrinkled brow to keep in mind all of the things which they have been told. As I watched their efforts, I have often wondered just how I would go about teaching golf. I like this book because it conveys my ideas of how golf should be taught. It has been approached from an average golfer's viewpoint.

Ed Acree is convinced that there is too much detail in teaching. He knows that all of us should understand the basic principles, and that the details will vary with one's physical conformation. After years of trials and tribulations, Jock and Bill Hutchison are able to standardize their games, and in this book Ed Acree has brought their technical information to a great degree of simplicity. He has presented those rules of play which are most helpful.

I have often played with Jock Hutchison. In this book he has passed along to the public all of his most interesting golden rules. He has played the game with such distinction that the whole golfing world has his performance impressed upon its memory. It has always been a matter of surprise to me that Bill Hutchison has not written *his* ideas on how to play golf, for he is one of the finest golf instructors in the game. He is pleasant, well educated, capable, patient, courageous, sympathetic, faithful, and honest. I would particularly select him.

Golf, of course, is a difficult game. I have never achieved a good result by hitting a ball carelessly. Perhaps I could make a distinction and say that one should hit the ball in a carefree way, but not carelessly. Golf does require concentration and thought.

My recipe for playing better golf is this: get the general idea of the game from this splendid book with its good understanding of the fundamentals; then select a few of the golden rules from Ed Acree's book after reading it, and practice the advice. The *average* golfer who hopes to be a *good* golfer can not dispense with the excellent instructions in this book.

CHARLES "CHICK" EVANS, JR.

TABLE OF CONTENTS

GOLF SIMPLIFIED

1. INTRODUCTION

GREETINGS, Brother Hackers. Welcome to the Rough and Divot Club. Before starting out to explore the rough and to dig a few fancy divots, let us take a minute to find out who wrote this book, what they know about golf, and what it contains which might help to improve your game.

It was written by a business man who started out as a beginner and who improved rapidly by means of a scientific approach to the game. Because the methods used have proven successful, he desires to give other golfers the benefit of them. Having suffered the agony of being possessed with a strong desire to play good golf, but lacking the skill to do so, has prompted his sincere desire to help other golfers improve their skill. He has persistently championed the cause of the average golfer.

During the process of development, he experienced having the jitters on the first tee and has suffered the embarrassment of having missed the ball completely. He has explored that part of the rough which is known as the "Bear Country" and has dug divots which would be a credit to atomic power. In fact, he was just a plain "dub." No matter how badly you play, he has played just as badly or worse. But from this experience, he knows that you too will play better golf, if the correct methods are used.

The technical information about golf has been supplied by Jock Hutchison, former British Open Champion, and Bill Hutchison, who has been an outstanding professional instructor for many years. Both are associated with the Glenview Club, Golf, Illinois, a suburb of Chicago. It has been reviewed by

1

"Chick" Evans, several times winner of the National Amateur Championship of the United States, who added his comments. *It represents combined expert opinion.*

Many instructors advise the use of written instructions; they know that written instructions are of considerable aid in the progress of those being instructed. Frequently, instructors limit the scope of instructions in order to avoid confusion. They appreciate the difficulty of trying to remember all of the information which is conveyed by the instructor within the limited time that they are together.

An early understanding of the elementary phases of instructions, by those being instructed, enables the instructor to concentrate on the advanced phases of the game. For that reason, those receiving instructions will aid their own progress by using written instructions, in so far as they are practical. *Written instructions should have the approval of the instructor when they are used as a complement to personal instructions.*

In an article appearing in the September, 1932, issue of the *American Golfer,* entitled "How Written Instructions Help," Bobby Jones says: "Of course, no one claims for instructive writing the benefits which can be gained from competent personal instruction. But I do think that instructive literature does serve a purpose; does have its place in the game. First, as a complement to personal instruction in bettering the pupil's understanding of the reasons for the motions he has gone through, and second, as a means of educating him in the game."

Bobby Jones was one of the outstanding players of all time. His success was not merely luck. It resulted from the use of scientific methods and the proper application of sound fundamentals. Other good players have adopted the same technique to improve their game. In view of their success, wouldn't it be wise for you to use written instructions as a means of helping to improve your game?

Several good books and articles on golf have been published. They contain a lot of valuable information; they have done much to promote a better understanding of golf; a lot of helpful information has been conveyed to those endeavoring to improve their game. The professionals, instructors, and authors are to be commended for their contribution. It has materialized in the playing of better golf. Particularly so, by golfers of the average class.

The author and his associates have approached this book with the objective of presenting the essentials of golf in clear and understandable form. The publication of it was undertaken in response to the many urgent requests to have it presented in book form after publication of the original material as a series of articles by *The Field Glass* and *The Hudsonian,* which are, respectively, the employee publications of Marshall Field & Company, Chicago, and the J. L. Hudson Company, Detroit.

It has been the sincere desire of the author and his associates to provide golfers with the essential fundamentals of the game, and to present these in such a manner as to be of help to them in playing better golf. They wish they could give golf enthusiasts some short-cut method of improvement, but honesty compels them to admit their inability to do so. *No one else can.* Permanent improvement is not accomplished overnight or by methods other than the proper application of sound fundamentals. That is why the fundamentals which are presented in this book will help to improve the average golfer's game, if properly applied. The degree of improvement will be in proportion to the degree in which they are consistently followed.

The material content has been condensed, organized, and presented in such form that it provides a useful, ready reference. There are many practical benefits to be derived from the use of a reference book. Especially so, by those engaged in business and professional activities who have many other things to think about between rounds of golf. *Keep it handy. Refer to it frequently.*

Occasionally we have to be reminded of the things which we already know. There are so many essential things about golf, which require the memory of players, that it is unreasonable to expect busy people to remember them without refreshing their memory occasionally. If golf consists of enough factors to write a book about it, the players have need for a ready reference book.

Successful athletic coaches have athletes attend "skull practice" frequently, in order to remind them of the essential points of the game. Similarly, golfers who expect to be successful should have "skull practice" occasionally to remind them of the fundamentals of golf.

That is the reason why this book provides the essential fundamentals of golf in such detailed and summary form that it serves as a quick and useful reminder for golfers whose interim activities between rounds of golf require their constant attention.

Come on, pals. Get your "shootin' irons." Let's explore the "Bear Country" and give atomic bombs some real competition in plain-and-fancy divot digging.

2. SCIENTIFIC APPROACH TO GOLF

A SCIENTIFIC method of approach to golf will contribute much to the success that individual players attain because of the effect which it has upon the development of mental attitude and physical ability. Proper mental attitude is a prerequisite to the development of physical ability. It directs the efforts to develop physical ability and provides the motivating force which is necessary to make these efforts produce successful results.

Before delving into the mechanics of a golf swing and the method of executing the various types of shots, possibly it might be well to consider the method of approach to golf from the standpoint of developing the proper mental attitude towards it.

An attempt to account for the large variation in the success attained by two golfers, who apparently are equal physically and comparable otherwise, reveals the importance of mental attitude. Mental attitude alone is not responsible for all of the difference, but it is a major factor. Physical condition, muscular co-ordination, nervous temperament, infrequent playing, and other things have an effect upon the type of golf which a person plays.

It would be impossible to describe all of the various types of attitudes toward golf and their effect upon the results which are obtained. But after excluding occasional players and those physically or otherwise handicapped, it is believed that some of the more common attitudes toward golf are portrayed by the following characters and descriptions:

Mr. I. N. Different. He insists that he plays golf for fun and is not concerned about the results. He makes no effort to improve his score. However, he likes the exercise and enjoys singing in the locker room quartette. He is convinced that if he took the game "seriously," he would be good at it. Maybe he would, but he is unwilling to admit his secret desire to play better golf and to exert the efforts which are necessary in order to do so. It is no coincidence that Messrs. Tee Jitters, M. Barrassment, and Hy Score are his constant companions.

Mr. I. Hope. He is on the lookout for some secret grip, new stance, or other miracle which will make him a top-flight golfer overnight. He takes golf seriously and would like to improve, provided it requires only a limited amount of effort and does not necessitate foregoing some of his pet ideas. He is willing to "try" something new once or twice, but when it fails to produce the miracle he has hoped for, it is soon discarded in favor of a pet idea. He is convinced that he was born to suffer—especially on a golf course. For some reason, Faith and Charity seem to desert him, but he has some other companions in Messrs. Lotto Grief, Con Fusion, and Duke I. Payoff.

Mr. A. Hard Trier. He is a fellow who really likes to play golf and has a sincere desire to improve. He devotes much time and effort in this attempt. He plays better than the average golfer. He has improved some as a result of his efforts, but the degree of improvement has not been in proportion to his efforts because of the lack of a scientific approach. Because of his conscientious efforts to improve, there is a good possibility that he will develop into a good golfer when and if he acquires a clear mental picture of the proper mechanics. His companions are not steady, but vary between Messrs. I. N. Consistent, Slim Satisfaction, and Count Dee Spondence.

Mr. B. A. Success. Here is a fellow who is sufficiently enthusiastic about golf to approach it scientifically. He makes it a point to find out "why" the clock ticks. First, he determines the factors which are of major importance, and then concentrates his major efforts on the mastery of those factors. Frequently he consults the club professional or a competent instructor in order to be sure that he is making the proper application of the correct methods. So it is only logical that Messrs. I. M. Steady, Lotto Pleasure, and King Confidence are his constant companions.

The preceding analysis emphasizes the importance of developing the proper mental attitude as the first step towards playing good golf. It is a step in the right direction. Once the first step has been taken, it is most likely that other constructive steps will follow.

One often wonders why a person spends so many years of his life attending school. What benefit does he derive? It increases his possibility of success in life because it provides the individual with a sense of direction. What benefit does a person derive from making a scientific approach to golf? He increases his possibility of success at golf because that approach provides him with a sense of direction. Fundamentally, both schooling and golf study are intended to serve the same purpose, for when a person attends school he *is only making a scientific approach to life.*

A scientific approach to golf is not an academic or high-powered theory. It is simply making practical use of a principle which has acknowledged merit, by applying it to golf. It is just good common sense that efforts which are directed and guided by definite objectives will produce better results, at a more rapid rate of progress, than efforts which are exerted without a purpose. In other words, even in golf, it pays you big dividends to know *where* you are going and *by what means* you intend to get there.

So many various factors have been introduced in connection with golf, that it is difficult for one to establish objectives which will serve as a guide in his efforts to improve. For example, the importance of relaxation and concentration has been stressed to a point where one would almost be justified to accept them as being the most important factors of golf. They are important factors, but from the standpoint of "relative importance," they do not compare equally with such factors as knowing the mechanics of the swing and mastering these mechanics.

As a matter of fact, relaxation and concentration are only incidental factors to the execution of a proper swing and the exercise of good judgment. They become important factors when combined with the proper mechanics, but it would not do much good to concentrate or relax unless the player is able to execute a correct swing or approximately thereto. Relaxation and concentration are important factors in flying an airplane, but they do not justify an attempt to fly one without proper knowledge of the mechanics which are involved.

Of course, no one could determine the exact ratio of relative importance which the individual factors involved bear to golf as a whole. The only way to estimate it is by using an arbitrary method of evaluation—no useful purpose would be served by determining the exact ratios. The important thing is to make a distinction between those factors which are of major importance and those which are of minor importance, so that the major efforts may be concentrated on items which are of major importance and that only minor efforts will be devoted to items which are of minor importance.

As a means of helping you to make that distinction, let us assume that if the factors involved were evaluated on an "arbitrary basis," they would be about as follows:

MECHANICAL FACTORS	RELATIVE IMPORTANCE
Knowledge of the mechanics which constitute a swing that is fundamentally sound and properly timed	40%
Mastery of the mechanics of a correct swing to the point where it is reproduced habitually and in the same manner each time it is executed	25%

OTHER FACTORS	
Judgment	10%
Confidence	10%
Concentration	5%
Relaxation	5%
Self-control	5%
	100%

Obviously, a knowledge of the mechanics and mastery of them are the most important factors in golf. The major effort should be devoted to them. Learning and mastering the mechanics will do more to develop the *other factors* than anything else.

The suggested steps for improvement at golf are as follows:

1. Develop a good mental attitude towards golf.
2. Learn the mechanics of a swing which is fundamentally sound and properly timed.
3. Master the mechanics of a correct swing to the point where it is reproduced habitually.
4. Exercise good judgment in selecting the type of shot to execute under the conditions which exist.
5. Refrain from worry and other things which prevent concentration and relaxation.

3. MECHANICS OF THE GOLF SWING

THE fundamental principle of achieving success in business is by the proper application of correct methods. Those who succeed because of rich relatives or political favoritism are exceptions, rather than the rule. The majority succeed because of sound principles. Success at golf is achieved by the proper application of correct methods. The degree of success will be in proportion to the degree in which the correct methods are properly applied.

Once the player has acquired a clear mental picture of the mechanics of a correct golf swing, much of the confusion about golf will be eliminated. Indecision, worry, and fear will disappear when that clear mental picture has been firmly established in the mind. Those negative factors are replaced by well-founded confidence.

A golf swing has been described as "a smooth, flowing motion without any mental or physical interruption." That is a good description of the swing. But, the best way to acquire a clear mental picture of the movements involved and their sequence is to divide the swing into stages.

The swing as it is used in play consists of eight major stages, which are:

1. Grip
2. Stance
3. Address
4. Backswing

5. Downswing
6. Impact
7. Follow through
8. Finish

The various stages of the swing constitute a portion of three separate and distinct functions which are logically classified as:

10

1. PREPARATION
    A. Grip
    B. Stance
    C. Address

2. EXECUTION
    A. Backswing
    B. Downswing
    C. Impact
    D. Follow through

3. FINISH

Thinking of the functions involved in the above listed order will simplify the application of mechanics in actual play. It will clarify the player's approach because it reduces the number of things which he has to think about at one time and centers the attention on major functions, instead of minor details.

An explanation of and comments about the various stages of the swing are given here.

GRIP

The most important features of the grip are:

1. *Type*. The overlapping grip is described here because it is used by a majority of the leading players. The use of it is suggested. However, many good players use the interlocking grip. If one uses the interlocking grip and it works satisfactorily, one should continue to use it.

   The use of a full right hand grip is suggested for players who have small hands. A high percentage of women players would play better golf if they used a full right hand grip.

2. *Intended purposes*. The intended purposes of the grip are:

   A. To permit free and uniform hand action throughout the swing.

   B. To insure a solid contact of the clubhead with the ball.

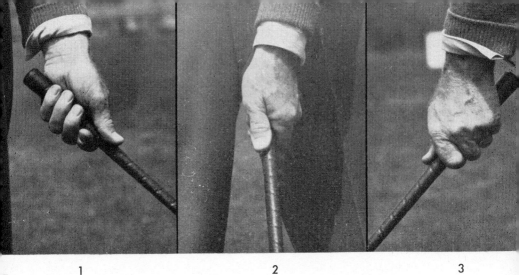

1   2   3

C. To have the clubface at the proper angle when it
   strikes the ball.

3. *Method of forming the grip.* Follow this sequence of
   action in forming the grip:

A. Hold the club near the end of the handle with the
   left hand. Place the clubhead on the ground, in its
   natural position, directly in front of the body.

B. Turn the left hand slightly over to the right. Grasp
   the top portion of the club shaft (near the end of
   handle) firmly, but not tightly, with the entire left
   hand.

C. Extend the left thumb down the top inside portion
   of the club shaft.

D. Place the middle portion of the right fingers underneath the club shaft, with the right little finger overlapping the left forefinger.

7   8   9

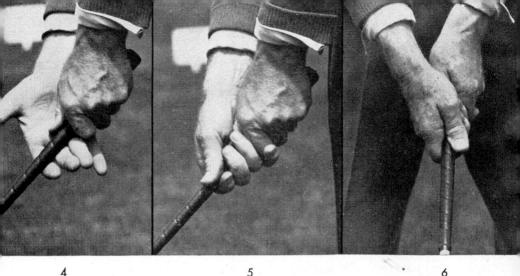

    E. Close the right hand so that the left thumb fits into the pocket formed by the upper palm of the right hand.

    F. Keep the grip firm, but not tight, and the hands close together.

4. *Pressure. There should be no pressure in any part of the grip.* If the grip is too tight, it will prevent free hand action and cause excessive shoulder action. If the grip is too loose, it will prevent solid contact with the ball.

5. *Comments.*

    A. The grip should remain firm throughout the swing without any voluntary tightening or loosening. An involuntary tightening at impact always occurs.

    B. The left thumb should be directly underneath the shaft, at the end of the backswing. A test of the grip used should be made during practice to see that it is.

10

GRIP

Figs. 1, 2, and 3. Take a full grip with the left hand. Extend the left thumb down the top inside portion of the clubshaft.

Fig. 4. Place the middle portion of the right fingers underneath the clubshaft, with the right little finger overlapping the left forefinger.

Figs. 5, 6, and 7. Close the right hand so that the left thumb fits into the pocket formed by the upper palm of the right hand.

Figs. 8, 9, and 10. Keep the grip firm, but not tight, and the hands close together.

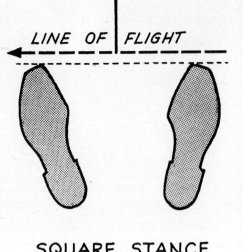

SQUARE STANCE

Both feet are equidistant from an imaginary line, which would be parallel to the intended line of flight.

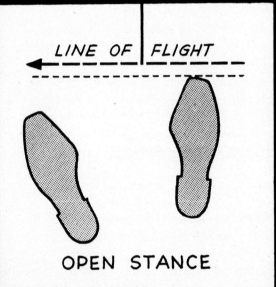

OPEN STANCE

The left foot is slightly withdrawn from an imaginary line, which would be parallel to the intended line of flight.

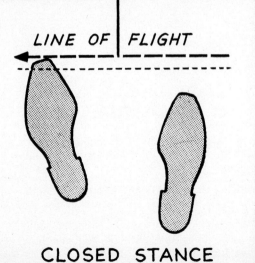

CLOSED STANCE

The left foot is placed nearer to an imaginary line, which would be parallel to the intended line of flight, than the right foot.

NARROW STANCE

The feet are placed close together.

WIDE STANCE

The feet are placed wide apart.

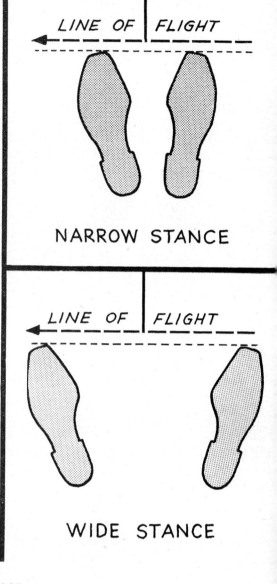

LINE OF FLIGHT

NARROW STANCE

LINE OF FLIGHT

WIDE STANCE

STANCE

The more important features of the stance are:

1. *Types.* As a means of explanation, the various types of stances commonly used are:

    A. Square Stance: Both feet are equidistant from an imaginary line, which would be parallel to the intended line of flight.

    B. Open Stance: The left foot is slightly withdrawn

from an imaginary line, which would be parallel to
the intended line of flight.

C. Closed Stance: The left foot is placed nearer to an
imaginary line, which would be parallel to the intended line of flight, than the right foot.

D. Narrow Stance: The feet are placed close together.

E. Wide Stance: The feet are placed wide apart.

An open stance is preferable for short iron shots where loft
is the desired factor or for shots where a slice is desired. A
square stance or a slightly open stance is preferable for other
shots. Many good players use a slightly closed stance for long
wood shots or where a hook is desired. The approximate width
of the stance and location of the ball for each shot are indi-
cated in Chapters 6 and 7.

2. *Intended Purpose.* The type of stance taken should provide good balance, be comfortable, and provide a firm
footing. It should permit an easy shift of the weight to
the right leg.

3. *Method of taking stance.* The steps to be followed in
taking the stance are:

A. Take a natural stance opposite the ball, with the
weight evenly divided on the ball and heel of each
foot.

B. Place the feet so that a line drawn across the toes
would be parallel to the intended line of flight. Turn
the toes slightly *outward.*

C. Bend the body slightly forward at the waist.

D. Keep the legs straight with the knees relaxed.

E. Let the hands hang in a natural position immediately
in front of the body.

4. *Width of stance.* The general principles which are followed in determining the width of the stance are:

A. To keep the feet close together on short shots.

B. To increase the width between the feet in proportion
to the increased distance of the shot, as the shots
become longer, until the maximum of shoulder-
width is reached.

C. The weight will not shift properly if the stance is *too* wide because it locks the hip action.

ADDRESS

The address of the ball is the last phase of preparation before executing the shot. All final adjustments of the body stance, grip, and clubhead are made at this point. All thoughts pertaining to the swing or execution of the shot should be made *before* starting the backswing.

1. *Manner of address.* The manner of address for a shot which requires a full swing is as follows:

   A. Stand opposite the ball, with the feet at right angles to the intended line of flight. Turn the toes slightly outward.

   B. Bend the body slightly forward at the waist. (Avoid the tendency to bend the body forward excessively.)

   C. Have the legs straight, but free at the knees.

   D. Let the hands hang naturally, immediately in front of the body, slightly ahead of the clubhead.

   E. Keep the grip firm, but not tight.

   F. Place the clubhead on the ground, in its natural position, immediately behind the ball and at right angles to the intended line of flight. Have the center of the clubface directly behind the ball.

   G. Start the backswing soon after the clubhead has been placed behind the ball.

   It is suggested that a few waggles of the club be made while addressing the ball as a means of preventing tension and to get loosened up.

2. *Location of the ball.* The general guides in determining the approximate location of the ball are these:

   A. Distance of body from the ball: For long shots, keep the hands low and fairly close to the body, as at address. Place the clubhead on the ground, in its natural position, directly in front of the body. The center of the clubface designates the approximate

1

2

3

spot where the ball is located. From a ball placed in that location, the player can determine the approximate distance away from the ball to stand when that club is used. For short shots, stand closer to the ball, as the shots become shorter.

If the player stands too close to the ball, the hands and arms will not function properly, and it is probable that the ball will be hit on the heel of the club. If the player stands too far away from the ball, it results in bending the body forward excessively, reaching for the ball, and hitting the ball on the toe of the club.

B. Relation of ball to the body: The location of the ball for short shots is slightly to the right of the center point between the feet. As the shots become longer, the position of the ball is gradually moved forward until, for shots which require the maximum distance, it is well to the left of the center point between the feet.

The approximate location of the ball for each shot is described later in Chapters 6 and 7.

STANCE AND ADDRESS

Fig. 1. Putts

Fig. 2. Chip Shots

Fig. 3. Pitch Shots

BACKSWING

The important features of the backswing are:

1. *Types of backswing.* FLAT ARC—used when executing shots which require distance. SEMI-FLAT ARC—used when executing shots which require a combination of distance and loft. UPRIGHT ARC—used when executing shots which require loft.

   The player should not attempt to execute a particular type of backswing. Usually the arc is determined by the width of the stance and the amount of body turn. A wide stance, with a considerable amount of body turn, usually produces a flat arc in the backswing.

   A stance of medium width, with a medium amount of body turn, usually produces a semi-flat are in the backswing.

   A narrow stance, without much body turn, usually produces an upright arc in the backswing.

2. *Intended purpose.* The intended purpose of the backswing is to get the hands and other parts of the body in a position to supply a sufficient amount of

4

5

6

STANCE AND ADDRESS

Fig. 4. Medium Iron Shots

Fig. 5. Long Iron Shots

Fig. 6. Wood Shots

power to propel the ball a required distance.

The player should be comfortable and have good balance at the end of the backswing.

It is advisable to test the balance during practice by raising the left foot off the ground and standing on the right foot only.

3. *Method of taking the backswing.* Here are the steps to follow in taking the backswing for a full swing:

A. Take the club straight back smartly, with the hands, to a position which is about ear high. (Both hands are used, but the left hand dominates the action.)

B. Keep the hands and wrists in their *same position* as at address, until about the half-way point in the backswing, when the wrists begin to bend backward. Continue to bend the wrists backward gradually, until they are fully cocked at the end of the backswing.

C. Keep the left arm extended during the backswing.

D. Simultaneously, as the hands start their backward swing, bend the left knee inward and raise the left heel. Most of the weight transfers to the right leg, and the hips turn to the right.

4. *General comments.* The backswing should be taken as one continuous, rhythmic action. All movements are smooth and properly synchronized.

BACKSWING

Figs. 1 and 2. The arms and hands take the club back smartly.

Fig. 3. The left knee bends inward and the left heel raises.

Fig. 4. Most of the weight transfers to the right leg. The hips turn to the right.

Fig. 5. The wrists begin to bend backward.

Figs. 6, 7, and 8. The arms and hands continue to take the club back. The wrists continue to bend backward.

Fig. 9. The left arm is extended. The clubshaft is parallel with the ground. Most of the weight has transferred to the right leg. Only the sole of the shoe underneath the big toe and the inside ball of the left foot touches the ground.

1   2   3

4   5   6

7   8   9

The transfer of weight and turn of the hips are not deliberate actions, but responsive actions. They respond almost automatically to the requirements of the hands for freedom of action in their backward swing.

At the end of the backswing, only the sole of the shoe underneath the big toe and the inside ball of the left foot touch the ground. The right leg is firm, the left arm fully extended, and the wrists are fully cocked. The left shoulder is slightly underneath. The clubshaft is parallel with the ground and pointing slightly to the left of the line of flight. The position of the clubhead is about halfway between pointing downward and facing upward (at about a 45° angle to the ground).

Because it is such an important phase of the swing, a considerable amount of time and effort should be devoted to the development of a proper backswing.

DOWNSWING

The important features of the downswing are:
1. *Amount of effort involved.* A substantial number of golfers add many strokes to their score because of their attempt to add increased power to their downswing.

DOWNSWING

Fig. 1. The arms and hands pull the club forward. The left heel returns to the ground and the right knee bends inward. Most of the weight transfers to the left leg.

Fig. 2. The hands lead the clubhead.

Fig. 3. The wrists straighten out. The right heel has started to raise.

1   2   3

The attempt to add force or power at the start of the downswing or during its progress usually results in less striking power, because it slows down the speed of the clubhead and prevents good timing.

It is the speed with which the clubhead strikes the ball that gives it distance. The speed of the clubhead is determined by the speed of the hands at the time of impact.

2. *Method of execution.* The movements to make in executing the downswing are:

   A. Keep the head and shoulders behind the swing. Start the downswing by a gradual pull of the hands toward the ball.

   B. Keep the hands and wrists in their *same original position,* as at the end of backswing, until impact, at which time the wrists uncock and straighten out.

   C. Keep the arms in close to the body during the downswing. (The right shoulder goes underneath.)

   D. As the hands approach the ball, return the left heel to the ground and kick the right knee inward. Most of the weight transfers to the left leg, and the hips turn to the left.

The return of the left heel to the ground, kicking the right knee inward, and the transfer of weight to the left leg are almost automatic actions. Particularly so, after a reasonable amount of practice.

3. *General comments.* It is essential that the head and shoulders stay behind the swing. The proper sequence and timing of the movements involved are important factors in the correct execution of the downswing. Practice and the elimination of attempts to add brute force or to throw the clubhead will help to develop a downswing which is reasonably correct.

IMPACT

The important things to do at the time of impact are:
1. Keep the head in its same original position.

2. Keep the hands moving fast without any attempt to add force or to steer the clubhead or to create other interference.

3. Keep the wrists in a *straightened-out* position. (Avoid the tendency to get the clubhead ahead of the hands, with a forward bend of the wrists. *The wrists remain straight.*)

IMPACT

The left arm is straight. The wrists are straightened-out. The head and shoulders are behind the stroke. The head stays down.

It is too late to help the flight of the ball at the time of impact. All the efforts to do so are in vain. The player should really turn loose and "let go" at impact.

FOLLOW THROUGH

The follow-through is that period from immediately after impact until near the finish. It does not affect the flight of the ball; it is a continuation of the swing. If it is not correctly executed, the probabilities are that the shot was not hit properly and that the cause originated in the previous stages of the swing.

The things to do in the follow-through are:

1. Keep the head in its original position until near the finish, when it turns slowly to the left from underneath. (Avoid the tendency to raise it upright, abruptly.)

1   2

FOLLOW THROUGH

Fig. 1. The hands continue to move fast and outwardly. The hips turn to the left.

Fig. 2. The head stays down until near the finish, when it turns slowly to the left from underneath.

2. Keep the hands moving fast and outward.

3. Keep the wrists in their *straightened-out* position until near the finish, at which time they bend forward.

4. The hips continue to turn to the left, the right knee bends inward, and the right heel raises.

All of these movements become automatic after a reasonable amount of practice.

FINISH

The finish is only a result and should not be of much concern to the player. It does not affect the flight of the ball. From the standpoint of golf mechanics, it serves to indicate the degree of correctness with which the swing has been executed.

A description of the finish of a full swing is as follows:

1. The head has turned to face the line of flight in order to follow the flight of the ball.
2. The body has turned around towards the line of flight.
3. Most of the weight has shifted to the left leg.

FINISH

The head and body have turned around to face the line of flight. The arms and wrists are relaxed. Most of the weight has transferred to the left leg. The right leg is relaxed with the knee bent forward and the heel upright.

4. The weight is supported mostly by the left heel and the outside portion of the ball of the left foot.
5. The right leg has relaxed, with the knee bent forward and the heel upright.
6. The hands are opposite to and slightly above the left shoulder, with the arms and wrists relaxed.
7. The clubshaft is behind the head, parallel to the shoulders and the ground. The toe of the club is pointing towards the ground. A state of relaxation and balance should exist at the finish.

TIMING AND RHYTHM

The top-flight golfers use their feet and knees in unison with the movement of their hands as a means of producing rhythm and timing in their swing and as a means of developing power.

Rhythm and timing result from co-ordination of the various

1   2   3   4

motions into their proper order and sequence. The maximum results are obtained with a minimum amount of effort by such co-ordination. In the final analysis, it simply means *doing the right thing at the right time.*

In a well-timed swing, the hands, feet, and knees move together in unison. For example, at the start of the backswing, while the hands take the club back, the left knee bends inward and the left heel raises.

Other examples of good timing are:

1. The wrists begin their backward bend at about the halfway point in the backswing.

2. The return of the left heel to the ground and kicking the right knee inward, as the hands start their downward swing.

3. Withholding any wrist action in the downswing until impact, when the wrists straighten out.

Attempts to add force or to apply the power of the stroke too early in the downswing distort the rhythm and timing of the stroke.

Because good foot and knee action are such important factors in the execution of a correct swing, it is well to develop them by means of exercise. Such exercise may be taken at home. Figs. 1-8 on this page illustrate the proper routine.

The suggested routine of exercise is:

1. Take a normal stance as though addressing a golf ball.

2. Bend the left knee inward and raise the left heel smart-

5   6   7   8

ly. Transfer most of the weight to the right foot and turn the left hip to the right.

3. Return the left heel to the ground, bend the right knee inward, and transfer most of the weight to the left leg.

Turn the right hip to the left and raise the right heel.

This exercise will develop good foot and knee action, which is all there is to that old "bugaboo" of golf, commonly referred to as the "pivot."

SOLID CONTACT WITH BALL

A solid contact of the clubhead with the ball is essential in the execution of all shots. Putts, chip shots, short pitch shots, and shots which require the maximum distance *must be stroked firmly*.

Firm wrists and a firm grip with the left hand at the time of impact will produce a solid contact with the ball, provided the clubface is at the proper angle.

SUMMARY

A summary of the full swing is as follows:

Preparation

The three stages of the swing which constitute the function of preparation, or make-ready, are:

GRIP

1. Place the clubhead on the ground, in its natural position, directly in front of the body. Turn the left hand over to the right, and grip the club near the end of the handle with a full left hand grip.

2. Extend the left thumb down the inside, top portion, of the club shaft.

3. Place the right hand well underneath the club shaft, with the right little finger overlapping the left forefinger. (Keep the right hand in a good hitting position.)

4. Keep the hands close together.

5. Maintain a firm grip during the swing, without any voluntary tightening or loosening.

STANCE

1. Take a stance which is natural and comfortable, with the weight evenly divided on the ball and heel of each foot.

2. Turn the toes slightly outward. (The feet are placed so that a line drawn across the toes would be approximately parallel to the intended line of flight.)

3. Bend the body slightly forward at the waist.

4. Keep the legs straight, but relaxed at the knees.

5. Let the hands hang in a natural position, immediately in front of the body.

The width of the stance should be the approximate width of the shoulders.

ADDRESS

1. Stand opposite the ball with the feet at right angles to the intended line of flight. (Turn the toes slightly outward.)

2. Bend the body slightly forward at the waist.

3. Keep the legs straight but free at the knees.

4. Let the hands hang naturally immediately in front of the body.

5. Play the ball from a location which is about halfway between the left foot and the center point between the feet.

6. Place the clubhead on the ground in its natural position, immediately behind the ball. Have the center of the clubface directly behind the ball.

7. Start the backswing soon after the clubhead has been placed behind the ball. Waggle the club a few times while addressing the ball, to loosen up.

Execution

The four stages of the swing which constitute the function of execution are:

BACKSWING

1. Take the club straight away from the ball, smartly, with the hands, to a position which is about ear high. (Use both hands, but let the left hand dominate.)

2. Keep the hands and wrists in the same position as at address, until about the halfway point in the backswing, when

1   2   3

7   8   9

13   14   15

4   5   6

10   11   12

16

PANORAMIC VIEW OF A FULL SWING

Panoramic View of a Full Swing with a Wood Club. Note that the Natural Body Stoop at Address is Maintained Until After Impact.

they begin to bend backward. Continue to bend the wrists backward gradually, until they are fully cocked at the end of the backswing.

3. Keep the left arm extended during the backswing.

4. Simultaneously, as the hands start their backward swing, bend the left knee inward and raise the left heel. Most of the weight transfers to the right foot and the hips turn to the right.

Only the inside sole of the shoe underneath the big toe and the ball of the left foot touch the ground at the end of the backswing.

DOWNSWING

1. Keep the head and shoulders behind the swing. Pull the hands gradually toward the ball.

2. Keep the hands and wrists in their *same original position* as at the end of the backswing, until impact, at which time the wrists "straighten out." (Let the hands lead the clubhead until impact.)

3. Keep the arms in close to the body during the downswing. (The right shoulder goes underneath.)

4. As the hands approach the ball, return the left heel to the ground and bend the right knee inward. Most of the weight transfers to the left leg and the hips turn to the left.

IMPACT

1. Keep the head in its same original position.

2. Keep the hands moving fast without any attempt to add force or to steer the clubhead or create other interference.

3. Keep the wrists in a *straightened-out* position. (Avoid the tendency to get the clubhead ahead of the hands at impact. *The wrists remain straight.*)

Turn loose and "let go" at impact.

FOLLOW THROUGH

1. Keep the head in its original position until near the finish, when it turns slowly to the left from underneath. (Avoid the tendency to raise the head *upright* abruptly.)

2. Keep the hands moving fast and outward.

3. Keep the wrists in their *straightened-out* position until near the finish, when they bend forward.

4. The hips continue to turn to the left, the right knee bends inward, and the right heel raises.

Finish

The finish constitutes the function of indicating the degree of correctness with which the swing has been executed. A description of the finish is as follows:

1. The head has turned to face the line of flight in order to follow the flight of the ball.

2. The body has turned around towards the line of flight.

3. Most of the weight has shifted to the left leg.

4. The weight is supported mostly by the left heel and the outside portion of the ball of the left foot.

5. The right leg has relaxed, with the knee bent forward and the heel upright.

6. The hands are opposite to and slightly above the left shoulder, with the arms and wrists relaxed.

7. The clubshaft is behind the head, parallel to the shoulders and with the ground. The toe of the club is pointing towards the ground. A state of relaxation and balance exists at the finish.

GENERAL

Use the knees and feet in unison with the movement of the hands to develop power and to produce rhythm. It is essential that the clubhead makes a solid contact with the ball. The deviations from a full swing are shown in Chapters 4 and 5.

4. FACTORS IN THE SWING

A S A FURTHER explanation of some of the important factors of golf and additional details about some of the motions which are involved in the execution of a golf swing, the following information is supplemental to the mechanics of a golf swing.

HAND ACTION

Good hand action combined with good foot and knee action is the essence of good golf. Because the hands hold the club, they are the controlling factor of each stroke. The power of the stroke is determined by the speed of the hands at the time of impact.

The hands should swing independently of the body. Otherwise, the speed of the hands will be reduced to the speed of the body, which is too slow to provide adequate distance for long shots. Players should always think of swinging their hands and try to develop good hand action. *A tight grip prevents good hand action.*

WRIST ACTION

There is not so much wrist action in the execution of a correct golf swing as the average golfer thinks. Excessive use of the wrists is a common fault among golfers. Excessive use of the wrists leads to rolling of the wrists and reduces the power of the stroke. If the wrists break too soon in the downswing, they destroy the power of the stroke. The main points to observe in using the wrists effectively are:

1. Avoid the use of excess wrist action in the backswing

and downswing.

2. Bend the wrists backward at about the halfway point in the backswing, without "rolling" them to the left or right.

3. Withhold the forward bend of the wrists in the downswing until impact.

The wrists should be *firm,* but *not* tense or tight.

SHOULDER ACTION

In a correct swing, the shoulder action follows the movements of the hands, knees, and feet. It should never take place ahead of the movement of the hands, knees, and feet. The left shoulder goes slightly underneath in the backswing. The right shoulder is slightly underneath in the downswing.

The action of the shoulders combined with the other movements is a factor in the development of power, but is *not an independent source of power.* Shoulder action is a natural following action rather than a conscious action. A slight turn of the shoulders is all that is necessary.

Excessive use of the shoulders usually results from one of the following reasons:

1. An attempt to add increased power to the stroke.

2. Lack of proper foot and knee action.

3. An attempt to take the club too far inside on the backswing.

Players should hit the ball with their hands instead of the shoulders.

FOOT AND KNEE ACTION

Good foot and knee action are essential in the development of power, rhythm, and balance. The left knee bends inward and the left heel raises in the early stages of the backswing. This action transfers most of the weight to the right foot and causes the left hip to turn to the right.

The left heel returns to the ground and the right knee bends inward in the early stages of the downswing. This action transfers most of the weight to the left foot and causes the right hip to turn to the left. The right heel begins to raise as a following action of bending the right knee inward.

The correct foot and knee action combined with the proper turn of the hips constitutes the so-called "pivot."

BODY TURN

The correct foot, knee, and hip action lead to a natural body and shoulder turn. The turn of the body does not affect the natural stoop of the body which occurs at the time of addressing the ball.

STRAIGHT LEFT ARM

Because the left arm controls the arc of the swing from the start of the backswing until well after impact, it must remain straight. While the left arm remains straight, it is never rigid except at impact, when it becomes involuntarily rigid.

Some of the common causes for bending the left arm are:
1. Gripping the club too tight.
2. Lack of wrist action.
3. *Attempting* to take the club back too far in the backswing.
4. *Attempting* to add increased power to the downswing or to guide the ball at impact.

The left arm should remain close to the body during the downswing.

OTHER FACTORS

Possibly the importance of factors not pertaining directly to golf mechanics might appear to have been under-evaluated in estimating the relative importance of all the factors. The other factors become secondary in importance only when compared with the mechanics of the swing. They represent the difference between two golfers of equal mechanical skill. Many major tournaments have been won because good judgment was exercised, or lost because poor judgment was exercised. Others have been won because of confidence, concentration, relaxation, and self-control, or lost because of a lack of them. *Do not underestimate their importance.*

Because judgment, confidence, concentration, relaxation, and self-control are intangible factors, they are difficult to explain; but a few informative remarks in connection with them may be of help here:

Judgment

Judgment means the ability to arrive at logical decisions by good mental processes after due consideration of all the factors which are involved. It is one thing which may mean the difference between a good round of golf and a bad one. In many instances it is the deciding factor between opponents. At golf, the individual players are *forced* to make decisions for *themselves*. They will succeed or fail in accordance with the type of judgment which they exercise.

During a round of golf, there are many things which require the individual player to exercise judgment. Some of the more common things to be determined are:

1. *The type of shot to execute under the conditions which exist.* Give due consideration to distance and loft requirements, hazards, wind, lie of the ball, and condition of the course and contour of the greens. Experience and keen observation are the best means by which to develop the habit of exercising good judgment in determining the type of shot to execute under the conditions which exist.

2. *The selection of a club with which to execute each shot.* After the type of shot to be executed has been determined, select a club which will provide the proper distance, loft, and roll. Give due consideration to personal skill with the various clubs, and recognize any limitations. Practice and experimenting with the various clubs will develop good judgment in selecting the proper club with which to execute each shot.

3. *Determination of distance.* Determination of distance by guess is hazardous. Reduce the possibility of error by com-

puting the approximate distance when possible. Deduct
the yardage shown on nearby fairway markers from the
total yardage shown on scorecards. Add or deduct the esti-
mated yardage between the spot where the ball is lying
and fairway markers. Examples of this method are:

Total yardage of hole, per scorecard	420 yd.
Less yardage shown on nearby fairway marker	200 yd.
Difference	220 yd.
Less estimated yardage of ball beyond marker	10 yd.
Approximate distance to the hole	210 yd.

Total yardage of hole, per scorecard	385 yd.
Less yardage shown on nearby fairway marker	200 yd.
Difference	185 yd.
Add estimated yardage of ball short of marker	15 yd.
Approximate distance to the hole	200 yd.

The ability to judge distance can be developed by forming a habit of estimating the distance between the spot
where the ball is lying and the green *before* computing
the approximate distance. It is important to learn to estimate distance fairly accurately without a guide because
there are many instances in which it is impossible to com-
pute the approximate distance.

Subsequent chapters contain information which will be helpful in the development of good judgment.

Confidence

Confidence is a state of feeling sure. Well-founded confidence
is a natural sequence to the development of skill. There is a
marked distinction between confidence and personal ego. Confidence which is well founded has merit. *It constitutes a basis
for decisive action.* Personal ego serves no worthwhile purpose.
It only encourages false hope from which disappointment

usually results. Only actual skill will give real confidence.

The only possible way to develop confidence at golf is to learn the mechanics of the swing and to master them to the point where they are habitually executed. Confidence will automatically result therefrom. Let it be repeated that *well-founded confidence is a natural sequence to the development of skill.*

Concentration

Concentration is simply centering the attention on one thing at a time in its proper order and excluding all other thoughts from the mind except those pertaining to the immediate problem at hand. The player must determine where to center his attention and what to concentrate on. For example, when walking up near a green which is to be played, the player should be studying the contour and speed of the green instead of thinking about how to get across the creek on the next hole. When getting ready to execute an approach shot to the green, the player should think about how to execute the mechanics necessary to get the ball onto the green, instead of attempting to visualize the flight of the ball onto the green.

Just center the attention on the next thing to be done and forget everything else. *Avoid mental daisy-picking.* Think about golf instead of wondering what your wife will have for dinner. Concentration is a matter of habit. It must be practiced in order to form the habit.

Relaxation

To relax is to maintain a state of normalcy. *Relaxation is natural.* It is interference that prevents relaxation. Once the player acquires the confidence which results from mastery of the mechanics, he will relax unless he is of a natural nervous temperament, tired, angry, or otherwise emotionally disturbed. Mental and physical relaxation go together. The same things affect both.

Get plenty of rest and avoid worry. When a player begins to tighten up, it is well for him to think of the pleasure angle of golf and to enjoy the companionship of fellow-players instead of attempting to score. Have all of the fun possible out of the game. After that has been done for a while, the player suddenly realizes that a state of relaxation exists.

A tight grip, holding on to the ground with the feet, and other things which create tension, are likely to prevent relaxation. Relaxation is accomplished by elimination of the things which interfere with it. Train yourself to relax by eliminating interference.

Self-control

Self-Control is a disciplinary measure which applies to golf in the same manner as in other things. *Anger is one of its worst enemies.* Do not lose your temper when you make a bad shot or something goes wrong. Establish objectives which are reasonable and expectations which are within your limits. Learn to accept a few bad shots and other difficulties in a philosophical manner.

When a player becomes angry, he usually loses several strokes. Throwing golf clubs and hitting the ground does not help. Such tactics represent poor sportsmanship. They create a bad impression with fellow-players. People dislike to play with players who throw clubs or otherwise display their anger.

The top-ranking professionals make poor shots occasionally. It is unreasonable for the average golfer to expect every shot to be perfect or nearly perfect. Try to make a good shot each time, but expect a few bad ones and accept them gracefully. Temperament has more bearing on self-control than anything else. Train yourself to maintain an even temperament under all conditions. Remember, whom the gods would destroy they first make mad.

The possibility of improving at golf and deriving more pleasure from the game by forming good mental habits is obvious. The degree of improvement and the added pleasure will be in proportion to the success of the training efforts.

5. MASTERY OF THE MECHANICS

A GOLFER is on the high road to success when the mechanics of a correct golf swing have been mastered to a point where the proper swing is executed habitually. He is free to concentrate on other things instead of having to "consciously" watch the details of the swing. In the final analysis, good golf is the result of forming the proper physical and mental habits.

One good method used to master the mechanics of the swing is to concentrate on one thing at a time; that is, master the grip first, then stance, address, backswing, and downswing in that order. After these factors have been mastered individually, they are co-ordinated into a well-timed swing and combined with the routine of address, which is to be used in play.

Of course, the best method used to develop and master the mechanics of the swing is to do so under the guidance of a competent professional instructor. It would be well for those who do not have access to competent professional instructors to study the written instructions and the illustrations carefully.

It is suggested that reference be made to the summary of the swing before practice of a full swing. Reference should be made to Chapters 6 and 7 which describe the method of executing the various types of shots before practice of the shorter swings.

Practice at swinging the club correctly will soon formulate good habits. One can practice in the backyard, on a vacant lot, or on a practice tee. Practice anywhere and anytime, except on the golf course while playing a game.

It is really fun to practice once one gets started doing it. Nearly all good golfers enjoy practice almost as much as they

41

do playing. It provides a fascination which one does not get from playing.

The value of practice cannot be overly emphasized. The benefits derived from purposeful practice are limited only by the degree of correctness with which the swing is executed. Players should not swing sloppily or hit balls aimlessly. They should attempt to swing correctly each time and hit each ball with a definite objective in mind.

It is just as easy to formulate correct habits as it is to formulate incorrect habits. The exercise of care in swinging a club or hitting a ball will help to formulate correct habits. Incorrect habits are formed by swinging sloppily or hitting balls aimlessly.

In order to establish a purposeful routine of practice the player must first determine what he hopes to accomplish by practice. Second, he must adopt a routine of practice which is designed to accomplish the desired objective. Some of the common objectives of practice and suggested routines follow.

Developing a Good Swing

The main purpose is to master the mechanics of a correct golf swing to the point where it is executed habitually. The practice routine should be designed to provide more time for swinging a club than is devoted to hitting balls. The routine should be followed until the player has formed the habit of executing a swing which is reasonably correct. As the player acquires a higher degree of skill at swinging a club, the amount of time devoted to the swing should be decreased and the time devoted to hitting balls should be proportionately increased.

A good method to follow in mastering the mechanics of a golf swing is to start with a very short swing and to practice it until it is mastered. Then try a swing which is a little longer and master that. Continue to graduate upward until the maximum length of a full swing is reached.

The idea is to start with short shots which require only the movement of the hands and arms, and to gradually increase the scope of hand action and to co-ordinate the hand action with the appropriate foot, leg, and body action at the various points in the swing until the maximum of a full swing is reached. Reference to the illustrations on hand action in Chapter 6 will show the gradual increase in the scope of hand action as the length of the swing is increased. The amount of foot, leg, and body action at the different points in the swing should be noted.

Improvement in Skill

The main purposes are to make minor adjustments in the swing and to develop skill in executing a particular type of shot.

MINOR ADJUSTMENTS IN THE SWING

The practice routine should be designed to devote a major portion of the time to hitting balls, with the attention centered on emphasizing the particular motion involved in the adjustment.

Only the adjustment of one motion should be attempted at one time unless the motions involved are very closely related. Adjustments or changes of other motions should be postponed until after the first adjustment has been mastered thoroughly. Occasionally, the adjustment of one motion automatically corrects the maladjustment of another motion.

DEVELOPING SKILL WITH A PARTICULAR SHOT

The practice routine should be designed to devote a good part of the time to practice of a particular type of shot.

Players should choose a shot which causes them to lose strokes while playing and practice it until they acquire a reasonable degree of skill in executing it. Shots from traps, bunkers, and the rough usually cause players to lose strokes while playing. Many strokes can be saved by practice of them. Players who hope to score well should practice the execution of short approach shots to the green and putts.

Retention of Skill

The main purpose is to retain skill in the use of all clubs. The practice routine should be designed so that one may devote a certain amount of time to the use of each type of club. It is well to start with short approach shots and gradually work up to the longer shots as one's skill improves.

Warm-up Session Before Playing

The main purpose is to get the feel of the clubs and to get the muscles loosened up for playing. The practice routines should be designed to devote a limited amount of time to hitting a few balls with a representative number of clubs. Players should spend a few minutes in the practice of putts before playing.

PRACTICE ROUTINES

Players who have difficulty in the execution of shots with a particular club should practice with it until they learn to use it. Players should become well acquainted with all of their clubs and stay acquainted with them by practice or frequent use. One rarely feels at ease among strangers; particularly so, on a golf course with a set of golf clubs which are complete strangers to the individual who is endeavoring to use them.

Practice routines should provide for rest periods and for checking points whereby players can test their progress. Players should establish practice sessions regularly, at given intervals. Set aside a certain amount of time each week to be devoted to practice, and use it.

The only known way to learn to play golf and to acquire skill at it is by practice. Once a player takes a bag of practice balls to a practice tee he has taken the first step in acquiring skill at golf. The chances are that he will discover the fascination of it and go a second time. After that it would be difficult to keep him away.

All golfers should adopt "practice makes perfect" as their theme song and *sing it loud and often*. It is not a bad number. Try it some time, after the locker room quartette has debased the strains of "Sweet Adeline" to a point where further endurance is intolerable. *Abide by the meaning of it.* By so doing you will find that golf offers many sources of pleasure in addition to those derived from healthful exercise in the open spaces, pleasant companionship, and singing in the locker room quartette.

6. EXECUTING ORDINARY GOLF SHOTS

FUNDAMENTALLY, the method of executing all golf shots is the same. In making short shots, the arc of the swing and the scope of action with the hands are decreased to correspond with the distance requirements. The amount of foot, knee, and body action employed is less than the amount employed in executing the longer shots. As the distance of the shots is increased, the arc of the swing becomes wider, the scope of action with the hands becomes greater, and more foot, knee, and body action is employed.

In order to provide a clear mental picture of how the hand, foot, knee and body action are increased in proportion to the increased distance requirements of each shot, the various types of shots are listed below in the order of their normal distance requirements.

> Putts
> Chip shots
> Pitch shots
> Medium iron shots
> Long iron shots
> Wood shots

Because there is considerable variation in the nature of shots which require consideration of additional factors, the method of executing them is described later under the caption of "special shots."

The player must plan each shot. The function of planning is used as a means of determining the type of shot to execute under the conditions which exist. A survey of the intended line of flight must be made in order to see what hazards, if any, are to be considered. The lie of the ball and the direction

1   2

Chip Shots

1   2

1   2

Long Pitch Shots

GRADUATION OF HAND AND BODY ACTION

Medium Iron Shots

1   2

Long Iron Shots

1   2

1   2

Wood Shots

and velocity of the wind must be considered. Selection must be made of a club which will provide the proper distance, loft, and roll, under the conditions which exist.

The methods of executing those shots which are more com-monly executed in a round of golf, are explained below.

PUTTS

Many golfers who play good golf from the tee to the green have difficulty with putts. However, there is no good reason why the average player cannot putt reasonably well. The men-tal phase of putting is almost as important as the physical phase. Mental strain, which develops tense nerves and tight muscles, probably causes more putts to be missed than are missed be-cause of defective physical mechanics.

Players usually relax and stroke the ball freely when exe-cuting the shots from the tee to the green because the require-ments for accuracy are not so exacting. But when confronted with the exacting requirements of putting the ball into a small hole, they become tense, tighten up, and fail to stroke the ball freely.

One cannot *wish* the ball into the hole. One must stroke the ball "sharply and firmly" in the direction of the hole if it is expected to go in. The player should adopt the philosophy that putts are only golf shots which should be executed in the same manner as other shots.

The adoption of a sound philosophy and the development of a smooth putting stroke—and plenty of practice—will cause a high percentage of the sinkable putts to drop in the hole.

Here is the recommended method for executing putts:

Planning

1. Survey the overall layout of the green in order to deter-mine the overall amount of slope from end to end and from side to side.
2. Survey the immediate area around the hole in order to determine the amount of slope in that area.
3. Survey the terrain in order to determine the potential

speed at which the ball will travel after being stroked.

4. Stand well behind the ball to view the line between the ball and the hole. (Also view the line of travel from the opposite direction on difficult putts, when it is practical to do so.)

5. Determine the best line of travel to the hole.

Preparation

1. *Grip*

Use the overlapping grip which has been described, with the following exceptions:

A. The left hand is not turned to the right.

B. The right hand is not so much underneath the handle of the clubshaft.

C. Both thumbs are on top of the clubshaft.

The steps to take in forming the grip for putts, are:

A. Grip the club with the left hand. Have the back of the left hand towards the hole.

B. Extend the left thumb down the top side of the handle portion of the clubshaft.

C. Place the right hand on the handle portion of the clubshaft so that the palm of the hand faces the hole.

D. Extend the right thumb down the top side of the handle portion of the clubshaft.

E. Have the right little finger overlapping the left forefinger.

Many good golfers use a reversed overlapping grip for the putting stroke in which the left forefinger overlaps the right little finger. Otherwise the two types of grips are the same.

2. *Stance.*

A. Take a natural, comfortable, and relaxed stance.

B. Place the feet fairly close together, at right angles to the intended line of travel.

C. Bend the body slightly forward at the waist.

D. Flex the knees slightly to prevent tension.

E. Keep the feet free without any attempt to hold on to the ground.

1   2   3   4

PUTTS — FRONT VIEW

Fig. 1. A comfortable stance with the clubhead **square** to the line of travel.

Fig. 2. Use the **hands** to take the club back.

Fig. 3. Keep the clubhead low.

Fig. 4. Stroke the ball **sharply and firmly** with the **hands**.

Fig. 5. Keep the hands moving forward, in the direction of the hole.

Fig. 6. Keep the head down until well after impact.

Fig. 7. The hands are well past the spot where the ball was lying, with the clubhead low and facing the hole.

5   6   7

    F. Let the hands hang natural, immediately in front of the body.

3. *Address.*

    A. Address the ball opposite to, and a few inches in front of, the inside part of the left foot.

    B. Keep the putter blade at right angles to the line of travel and parallel to the ground, with the clubshaft maintained almost upright.

    C. Place the center of the putter blade directly behind the ball.

Execution

1. *Backswing.*

    A. Take the club straight back with the hands to a distance which is only a few inches behind the ball. (A short backstroke on putts is preferable. The length of the backstroke is determined by the distance which the ball must travel.)

    B. Keep the putter blade close to the ground. (Avoid raising the putter blade by bending the wrists without moving the hands back. The *hands* take the club back. Very little wrist action is used.)

2. *Downswing.*

    A. Let the *hands lead the clubhead* in the forward stroke.

    B. *Pull* the hands forward, gradually.

    C. Stroke the ball *sharply and firmly* with the hands. (Avoid the tendency to try to steer or guide the ball. Stroke it *sharply* in the direction of the hole. It will go into the hole or be near to it, if stroked correctly.)

    D. Keep the hands moving forward in the direction of the hole. (The player should have the feeling that the hands are still leading the clubhead.)

    E. Keep the head in its original position until *well after impact,* when it turns slowly to the left from underneath.

Finish

At the finish, the putter blade is low and facing the hole. The hands are well past the spot where the ball was lying. The back of the left hand is toward the hole.

General

The player should attempt to roll long approach putts only close enough to the hole to make the next putt easy.

Summary

Here is a summary of the method of executing putts:

PLAN

1. Survey the contour and terrain of the green in order to determine its slope and potential speed.

2. Stand well behind the ball to view and to determine the line of travel.

PREPARATION

1. Take a firm but relaxed grip with both thumbs on the top side of the handle portion of the clubshaft.

2. Take a narrow stance which is natural, comfortable, and relaxed. Keep the feet and the knees free. Let the hands hang naturally, immediately in front of the body.

3. Address the ball opposite to the inside part of the left foot. Have the putter blade *square* with the line of travel and parallel to the ground, with the clubshaft almost upright. Place the center part of the clubhead directly behind the ball.

EXECUTION

1. Use a *short* backstroke. Take the club straight back with the *hands*. (Not the wrists only.) Keep the putter blade low.

2. *Pull* the hands forward, gradually. Stroke the ball *sharply and firmly* with the *hands*.

3. Keep the hands moving forward, in the direction of the hole.

4. Keep the head down until well after impact. *Stay down with the stroke.*

FINISH

The hands are well past the spot where the ball was lying. The clubhead is low and facing the hole. The back of the left hand is towards the hole.

1 2 3 4

PUTTS — SIDE VIEW
Figs. 1-4. Side view of the putting stroke.

GENERAL
The adoption of a sound philosophy about putts and practice of the correct stroke will develop confidence and good putting.

CHIP SHOTS
Chip shots are usually executed from near the edge of the green with a club which gives the ball a considerable amount of roll without much loft. The chip iron, or Nos. 4, 5, and 6 irons, are popular clubs with which to execute chip shots.

The simplicity of execution makes it a desirable shot to use when the ball is near to the edge of the green, if there are no hazards or abnormal loft requirements involved. A pitch shot, executed with a club which provides loft, is generally used to clear hazards.

The execution of chip shots is similar to the execution of long approach putts. The use of a club with a slight amount of loft on the clubface, using a little more backstroke, and striking the ball a sharper blow are the main differences. Always chip the ball onto the smooth surface of the green so that it will roll straight towards the hole.

Here is the suggested method for executing chip shots.

Planning
1. Stand a few feet back of the ball and face the green.
2. View the ground between the ball and the edge of the

1   2   3

CHIP SHOTS — FRONT VIEW

Fig. 1. A narrow stance with the hands slightly ahead of the club-head.

Fig. 2. Take the club back with the **hands**.

Fig. 3. Pull the hands forward **gradually**. Stroke the ball **sharply and firmly** with the **hands**.

Fig. 4. Keep the hands moving in the direction of the hole. Keep the head down until well after impact.

Fig. 5. The wrists are in a straightened-out position and the arms are extended at the finish.

4   5

green in order to determine the slope, length of grass, loft requirements, and other factors.

3. Consider the slope and the potential speed of the green to determine the likely course and speed of travel after the ball has been chipped onto the green.

4. Select a club without much loft on the face, unless the conditions require the use of a lofted club.

Preparation

1. *Grip.*

A. Place the clubhead in its natural position, in front of the body. Turn the left hand over to the right and grip the club with a full left hand grip.

B. Extend the left thumb down the inside grip-portion of the clubshaft.

C. Place the right hand underneath the grip portion of the clubshaft with the right little finger overlapping the left forefinger.

D. Keep the hands close together and maintain a firm but relaxed grip during the stroke.

2. *Stance*

A. Take a narrow, slightly open stance which is natural, comfortable, and relaxed.

B. Bend the body slightly forward at the waist. Keep the legs straight but free at the knees. Keep the feet free.

C. Let the hands hang naturally, immediately in front of the body.

3. *Address*

A. Play the ball from about the center point between the feet or slightly to the right thereof.

B. Place the clubhead *square* behind the ball, at right angles to the line of travel, with the clubshaft almost upright.

C. Have the center part of the clubface directly behind the ball.

Execution

1. Use a short backstroke. Take the club back with the *hands.*
2. Keep the clubhead low, close to the ground.
3. Let the hands lead the clubhead in the forward stroke.
4. *Pull* the hands forward, gradually.
5. Stroke the ball *sharply and firmly* with the *hands.* (Avoid the tendency to bend the wrists forward. Keep the wrists in a *straightened-out* position.)
6. Keep the hands moving in the direction of the hole.
7. Keep the head down until *well after impact,* when it turns slowly to the left, from underneath. (Stay down with the shot and continue the stroke.)

Finish

At the finish, the clubhead is low and facing the hole. The hands are well past the spot where the ball was lying. The wrists are in a straightened-out position and the arms are extended.

Summary

A summary of the method of executing chip shots is as follows.

PLAN

1. Stand behind the ball, face the green, and survey the terrain between the ball and the hole. Determine the line of travel and loft requirements.

2. Determine the slope and potential speed of the green.

3. Select a club which will provide the proper amount of loft and roll.

PREPARATION

1. Use the overlapping grip which has been described.

2. Use a narrow, slightly open stance which is natural, comfortable, and relaxed.

3. Play the ball from about the center point between the feet or slightly to the right thereof.

4. Place the clubhead *square* behind the ball, at right angles to the line of travel, with the clubshaft almost upright. Place

1   2   3

the center part of the clubface directly behind the ball.

5. Bend the body slightly forward at the waist. Keep the legs straight but relaxed at the knees. Keep the feet free. Let the hands hang naturally, immediately in front of the body.

EXECUTION

1. Use a short backstroke. Take the club straight back with the *hands*.

2. Keep the clubhead low, close to the ground.

3. Let the hands lead the clubhead in the forward stroke.

4. *Pull* the hands forward, gradually.

5. Stroke the ball *sharply and firmly* with the hands.

6. Keep the hands moving in the direction of the hole.

7. Keep the head down until well after impact. (Stay down with the shot and continue the stroke.)

FINISH

At the finish, the clubhead is low and facing the hole. The

4   5

CHIP SHOTS

Figs. 1-5. Side view of a chip shot.

hands are well past the spot where the ball was lying. The wrists are in a straightened-out position and the arms are extended.

PITCH SHOTS

Accuracy is the desired objective of pitch shots. Control of the ball is the feature which produces accuracy. Some pitch shots will permit a considerable amount of roll after being hit onto the green. Others require that the ball make a sudden stop after landing on the green. Use of the proper club and the correct execution of the stroke will provide the control features which produce accuracy.

As a general rule, a mashie-niblick (No. 7 iron) is used for long pitch shots and for short pitch shots which will permit a considerable amount of roll after the ball lands on the green. A niblick (No. 8 or 9 iron) is generally used for pitch shots that require a sudden stop of the ball after landing on the green. Some players use a pitching iron for executing pitch shots. Others use a sand wedge. The advantageous use of a sand wedge for pitch shots requires a favorable lie of the ball, practice with it, and continuous use of it.

In the execution of pitch shots, many players make the mistake of trying to help the club loft the ball by bending the wrists forward, or by use of some unnatural method of stroking the ball. Some players endeavor to play cut-shots by hitting from the outside in, or employ other methods to impart backspin, so that the ball will stop suddenly after landing.

Several years ago when the types of clubs made were limited to such a small number that clubs with ample loft and backspin were not provided, the efforts of players to produce loft and backspin were justified. But in recent years the clubmakers have designed clubs which, if properly used, will provide ample loft and backspin without requiring any help from the player or necessitating any unusual type of effort.

Ample loft and backspin will be acquired, if the player will:

1. Use a club with ample loft of clubface.

2. Take a narrow stance which is slightly open.

3. Play the ball from a location which is slightly to the right of the center point between the feet.

4. Execute a stroke which is reasonably correct, in a *natural* manner. (Just follow the method of executing pitch shots which is explained later.)

The method of executing pitch shots is as follows.

Planning

1. Stand well behind the ball and face the intended line of flight.

2. Survey the terrain between the ball and the green to determine the hazards and other factors which are involved.

3. Consider the direction and velocity of the wind, if any, to determine its probable effect upon the flight of the ball.

4. Survey the contour and terrain of the green to determine its slope and potential speed.

5. Select a club which will provide ample loft with the desired amount of backspin or roll, from that particular lie of the ball.

Preparation

1. Use the overlapping grip which has been described. (Keep the grip relaxed a little more for pitch shots than for other shots.)

2. Take a narrow, slightly open stance which is natural and comfortable. (The normal distance between the feet is about six to nine inches for short pitches and about nine to twelve inches for long pitches.)

3. Play the ball from about the center point between the feet or slightly to the right of the center point. (In some instances the location of the ball is further back towards the right foot to meet abnormal loft requirements or to make the ball raise immediately after being stroked.)

4. Have the hands slightly ahead of the clubhead at address. Place the center of the clubface directly behind the ball.

1   2   3

4   5   6

7   8   9

Execution

1. *Backswing*

    A. Take the club straight back smartly with the *hands*, to a position which is about waist high, for short pitches. (About shoulder-high for long pitch shots.)

    B. Keep the hands and wrists in the *same position* until near the end of the backswing, at which time the wrists bend slightly backward. (There is only a slight backward bend of the wrists on pitch shots.)

    C. Keep the left arm extended during the backswing.

    D. Simultaneously, as the hands start the backswing, bend the left knee inward and raise the left heel slightly. Most of the weight transfers to the right foot, and the left hip turns to the right.

2. *Downswing*

    A. Keep the head and shoulders *behind the stroke*. (This is essential in order to get the required loft.) *Pull* the hands forward, gradually.

    B. Keep the arms in close to the body.

    C. Keep the hands and wrists in their *original position*

SHORT PITCH SHOTS

Fig. 1. A slightly open stance with the hands slightly ahead of the clubhead.

Fig. 2. Take the club straight back smartly with the hands. The left knee bends inward and the left heel raises **slightly.**

Fig. 3. The wrists begin to bend backward. The left hip turns to the right.

Fig. 4. The left arm is extended.

Fig. 5. The hands lead the clubhead, the left heel returns to the ground, and the right knee bends inward.

Fig. 6. The wrists are in a straightened-out position at impact.

Fig. 7. The hands continue to move fast and outwardly.

Fig. 8. The head stays down until near the finish, when it turns slowly to the left from underneath.

Fig. 9. The head and body have turned around to face the line of flight. The arms are extended and the wrists are in a straightened-out position. Most of the weight has shifted to the left leg. The right leg has relaxed with the knee bent forward and the heel slightly raised.

1   2   3

as at the end of backswing until impact, at which time they *straighten out*.

D. As the hands approach the ball, return the left heel to the ground and kick the right knee inward. Most of the weight transfers to the left leg, and the right hip turns to the left.

3. *Impact*

A. *Keep the head down.*

B. Stroke the ball *sharply and firmly* with the hands.

C. Keep the hands moving fast without any attempt to *help* the clubhead loft the ball.

4. *Follow through*

A. Keep the hands moving fast and outwardly.

B. Keep the wrists in their *straightened-out* position.

C. The right hip turns to the left.

D. Keep the head in its original position until near the finish, when it turns slowly to the left from underneath.

7   8   9

4   5   6

LONG PITCH SHOTS

Fig. 1. A comfortable stance with the hands slightly ahead of the clubhead.

Fig. 2. The hands take the club straight back **smartly**. The left knee bends inward and the left heel raises.

Fig. 3. The wrists begin to bend backward. The hips turn to the right.

Figs. 4 and 5. The hands and arms continue to take the club back, and the wrists continue to bend backward.

Fig. 6. The left arm is extended.

Fig. 7. The hands lead the clubhead. The left heel returns to the ground and the right knee bends inward.

Fig. 8. The wrists straighten out.

Fig. 9. The hands continue to move fast and outwardly.

Fig. 10. The hips turn to the left.

Fig. 11. The head stays down until near the finish, when it turns slowly to the left from underneath.

Fig. 12. The head and body have turned around to face the line of flight. The arms and wrists are relaxed. Most of the weight has shifted to the left leg. The right leg is relaxed, with the knee bent forward and the heel upright.

10   11   12

1   2   3   4

FOOT AND LEG ACTION — LONG PITCH SHOTS

Fig. 1. The weight is evenly balanced at address.

Figs. 2 and 3. The left knee bends inward and the left heel raises in the early stages of the backswing.

Fig. 4. Most of the weight has transferred to the right leg. Only the sole of the shoe underneath the big toe and the inside ball of the left foot touches the ground at the end of the backswing.

Figs. 5, 6, and 7. The left heel returns to the ground and the right knee bends inward as the hands approach the ball in the downswing.

Fig. 8. Most of the weight has shifted to the left leg. The right leg is relaxed, with the knee bent forward and the heel upright.

5   6   7   8

Finish

1. The head has turned to face the line of flight in order to follow the flight of the ball.
2. The body has turned around to face the line of flight.
3. Most of the weight has shifted to the left leg.
4. The weight is supported by the left heel and the outside portion of the ball of the left foot.
5. The right leg has relaxed, with the knee bent forward and the heel raised slightly.
6. On short pitch shots the hands are about waist high, the arms are extended well forward in the direction of the hole, with the wrists in a *straightened-out* position. On long pitch shots the hands finish about shoulder high, well in front of the body, with the arms and wrists relaxed.

General

The main thing is to execute a normal stroke which is natural enough to keep the weight of the body behind the stroke. Let the clubhead do the work which it was designed to do. The clubhead will do its work better *without any help from the player.*

Summary

A summary of the method of executing pitch shots follows.

PLAN

1. Stand behind the ball and face the line of flight in order to survey the terrain and green for hazards and slope.
2. Select a lofted club which will provide the desired amount of backspin or roll, from that particular lie of the ball.

PREPARATION

1. Use the normal overlapping grip. Keep it relaxed.
2. Take a narrow, slightly open stance with the body bent slightly forward and the knees relaxed.
3. Have the hands slightly *ahead* of the ball, at address. Place the center of clubface directly behind the ball.

EXECUTION

1. Take the club straight back *smartly* with the *hands,* to a position which is about waist high, for short pitches. (About

shoulder high for long pitches.)

2. Bend the left knee inward and raise the left heel slightly. Most of the weight transfers to the right leg and the left hip turns to the right.

3. Bend the wrists backward, slightly, near the end of the backswing.

4. Keep the head and shoulders *back* of the stroke. *Pull* the hands forward gradually.

5. Keep the arms in close to the body. Let the hands lead the clubhead until impact, when the wrists *straighten out*.

6. As the hands approach the ball, return the left heel to the ground and kick the right knee inward. Most of the weight transfers to the left leg.

7. Stroke the ball *sharply and firmly* without any attempt to help the clubhead loft the ball.

8. Keep the wrists in their *straightened-out* position and the hands moving fast and outwardly. The right hip turns to the left.

9. Keep the head in its original position until near the finish, when it turns slowly to the left, from underneath.

FINISH

1. The head and body have turned to face the line of flight.

2. The weight has shifted to the left leg and is supported by the heel and the outside of the ball of the left foot.

3. The right leg has relaxed with the knee bent forward and the heel raised slightly.

4. On short shots the hands are about waist high and the arms extended well forward, in the direction of the hole, with the wrists in a straightened-out position. On long shots the hands finish about shoulder high, well in front of the body, with the arms and wrists relaxed.

MEDIUM IRONS

The use of medium irons (Nos. 4, 5, and 6) requires accuracy and a certain amount of distance. Accuracy should be the first consideration of the player, because obtaining greater distance only requires the use of a stronger club.

Obtaining the proper distance is just as important as obtaining the proper direction, but the method of obtaining the proper distance is much simpler. Usually, it only requires the use of a stronger or weaker club, or stroking the ball harder or easier.

A combination of several factors is required to obtain accuracy. The stance, the plane of the swing, and the angle at which the clubface strikes the ball affect the direction of its flight.

The stance should encourage the swing of the hands *towards* the hole. At address, the clubhead should be placed at right angles to the line of flight. The stroke should be executed in such manner that at impact the angle of the clubface is *square* to the line of flight.

Clubs should be used for distances which are within their normal range. Attempts to acquire distance beyond their normal range usually produce poor results because of the player's effort to hit the ball *hard*. This is commonly referred to as *pressing*.

The use of clubs for less than their normal distance range usually results in stroking the ball *too easily* and *quitting* before the stroke is completed. The length of the swing should be *decreased* and the ball stroked *sharply and firmly* when clubs are used for distances which are less than their normal range.

The method of executing medium iron shots is as follows.

Planning
1. Stand well behind the ball and face the line of flight.
2. Survey the terrain along the intended line of flight for hazards or obstructions. Note the overall contour of the . green. Avoid shooting over hazards, where feasible.
3. Consider the direction and velocity of the wind in order to determine its probable effect upon the flight of the ball.
4. Select a club which will provide the proper loft and distance from that particular lie of the ball.

Preparation
1. Use the overlapping grip which has been described, and keep the wrists firm.

1   2   3

2. Take a slightly open, comfortable stance of medium width. (Normally the feet are about 12 to 15 inches apart.)
3. Play the ball from about the center point between the feet.
4. Place the hands ahead of the clubhead and the center of the clubface directly behind the ball.

Execution

1. *Backswing*
   A. Take the club straight back *smartly* with the *hands,* to a position which is about eye-high.
   B. Keep the hands and wrists in their original position as at address, until about the halfway point in the backswing, when the wrists begin to bend backward.
   C. Continue to bend the wrists backward until they are fully cocked, at the end of the backswing.
   D. Keep the left arm extended during the backswing.

7   8   9

4   5   6

MEDIUM IRONS

Fig. 1. A comfortable stance with the hands slightly ahead of the clubhead.

Fig. 2 The hands take the club straight back **smartly.**

Fig. 3. The left knee bends inward and the left heel raises.

Fig. 4. The wrists begin to bend backward. The hips turn to the right.

Fig. 5. The hands and arms continue to take the club back. The wrists continue to bend backward.

Fig. 6. The left arm is extended.

Fig. 7. The arms and hands pull the club forward, gradually. The left heel returns to the ground, and the right knee bends inward.

Fig. 8. The hands lead the clubhead.

Fig. 9. The wrists straighten out.

Fig. 10. The hands continue to move fast and outwardly. The hips turn to the left.

Fig. 11. The head stays down until near the finish, when it turns slowly to the left from underneath.

Fig. 12. The head and body have turned around to face the line of flight. The arms and wrists are relaxed. Most of the weight has shifted to the left leg. The right leg is relaxed, with the knee bent forward and the heel upright.

10   11   12

E. Simultaneously, as the hands start the backswing, bend the left knee inward and raise the left heel. Most of the weight transfers to the right leg and the hips turn to the right.

2. *Downswing*
    A. Keep the head and shoulders *behind the swing. Pull* the hands forward gradually.
    B. Keep the hands and wrists in their same original position, as at the end of backswing, until impact, at which time they *straighten out.*
    C. Keep the arms in close to the body.
    D. As the hands approach the ball, return the left heel to the ground and kick the right knee inward. Most of the weight transfers to the left leg.

3. *Impact*
    A. Stroke the ball *sharply and firmly* with the *hands.*
    B. Keep the hands moving fast without any attempt to *help* the clubhead loft the ball.
    C. Keep the left arm straight and the head down.

4. *Follow through*
    A. Keep the hands moving fast and outwardly.
    B. Keep the wrists in their *straightened-out* position.
    C. The hips turn to the left.
    D. Keep the head in its same original position until near the finish, when it turns slowly to the left, from underneath.

Finish

1. The head has turned to face the line of flight in order to follow the flight of the ball.
2. The body has turned around to face the line of flight.
3. Most of the weight has shifted to the left leg.
4. The weight is supported by the left heel and the outside portion of the ball of the left foot.
5. The right leg has relaxed with the knee bent forward and the heel upright.

1 2 3 4

FOOT AND LEG ACTION — MEDIUM IRON SHOTS

Fig. 1. The weight is evenly balanced at address.

Fig. 2. The left knee bends inward and the left heel raises in the early stages of the backswing.

Fig. 3. Most of the weight has transferred to the right leg. Only the sole of the shoe underneath the big toe and inside the ball of the left foot touches the ground at the end of the backswing.

Fig. 4. The left heel returns to the ground and the right knee bends inward as the hands approach the ball in the downswing.

Fig. 5. The left heel is on the ground, and the right heel has started to raise at impact.

Fig. 6. The right knee continues to bend inward, and the right heel continues to raise.

Fig. 7. The hips turn to the left, and the right heel continues to raise.

Fig. 8. Most of the weight has transferred to the left leg. The right leg has relaxed, with the knee bent forward and the heel upright.

5 6 7 8

6. The hands are opposite to and slightly above the left shoulder. The arms and wrists are relaxed.

7. The shaft of the club is over the left shoulder and parallel with the ground. The toe of the club is pointing towards the ground.

General

It is well to remember that medium irons were designed for loft and a reasonable amount of distance. They should be used within the limits of their normal range. Other clubs were designed to provide greater distance.

Summary

Here is a summary of the method of executing medium iron shots:

PLAN

1. Stand behind the ball to survey the line of flight and the overall contour of the green. Consider the direction and velocity of the wind, if any.

2. Select a club which will provide the required loft and distance from that particular lie of the ball.

PREPARATION

1. Use the overlapping grip which has been described. Keep the wrists firm.

2. Take a stance of medium width, which is slightly open and comfortable. Play the ball from about the center point between the feet.

3. Place the hands slightly ahead of the clubhead and the center of the clubface directly behind the ball. Have the clubhead *square* to the line of flight.

EXECUTION

1. Take the club straight back, *smartly* with the *hands,* to a position which is about eye-high.

2. Keep the hands and wrists in their same position until about the halfway point in the backswing, when the wrists gradually begin to bend backward. Keep the left arm extended.

3. As the hands start the backswing, bend the left knee inward and raise the left heel. Most of the weight transfers to

the right leg and the hips turn to the right.

4. Keep the head behind the swing. *Pull* the hands forward gradually. Let the hands lead the clubhead until impact, when the wrists *straighten out.* Keep the arms in close to the body.

5. As the hands approach the ball, return the left heel to the ground and kick the right knee inward. Most of the weight transfers to the left leg and the hips turn to the left.

6. Stroke the ball *sharply and firmly* with the *hands,* without any attempt to *help* the clubhead loft the ball. Keep the head down, left arm straight, and the hands moving fast and outwardly.

7. Keep the wrists in their straightened-out position until near the finish, when they gradually bend forward.

FINISH

1. The head and body have turned to face the line of flight. Most of the weight has shifted to the left leg and is supported by the heel and outside of the ball of the left foot. The right leg has relaxed with the knee bent forward and the heel upright.

2. The hands are opposite to and slightly above the left shoulder. The arms and wrists are relaxed.

3. The clubshaft is over the left shoulder and parallel with the ground. The toe of club is pointing towards the ground.

LONG IRONS

Distance and direction are the main objectives of long irons (Nos. 2 and 3). More players seem to have more difficulty in using long irons than any of the other clubs. There are three possible reasons why this is so. First, they overswing. Probably so, because a longer clubshaft makes them feel that they should take an abnormally long backswing and "wallop" the ball.

Second, they attempt to hit the ball too hard, because a considerable amount of distance is required. Third, they try to help the club loft the ball, because the clubface appears to provide very little loft.

Fundamentally, long irons are no different from the other

iron clubs. There are no reasons why the swing should be changed when they are used. Despite the fact that the shaft is a little longer and the clubface is not lofted as much, they are still iron clubs and should be used as such.

A firm left wrist is maintained on *all iron shots*. Long iron shots are planned and executed in the same manner as medium iron shots, with the following modifications:

1. Stand a little farther away from the ball.
2. The location of the ball is slightly to the left of the center point between the feet.
3. The stance is a little wider.
4. The hips and body turn a little more in the backswing.
5. The backswing is slightly longer. (Only slightly longer.)

The above modifications apply to shots executed with a No. 1 driving iron, which are usually made from a tee with the ball teed up. Some players use the No. 1 iron advantageously from the fairway when playing against a strong wind.

WOOD SHOTS

Many golfers find that it is easier to execute shots with wood clubs than with iron clubs. The probable reason is that players relax and stroke the ball more freely when distance and reasonably good direction are the requirements of the shots, whereas iron shots require a high degree of accuracy which causes many players to tighten up and try to "steer or guide" the ball into a precise line of direction.

Those who have difficulty with wood shots may attribute it to one or more of the following reasons:

1. They endeavor to hit the ball too hard from off the tee.
2. They try to help the clubhead loft the ball from off the fairway.
3. They get too much body action in their swing. (If the body leads the hands in the downswing it usually produces a smothered shot or a slice.)
4. They close the clubface too much by use of an incorrect grip, by poor wrist action, or by using the right hand too much.

A reasonable amount of distance will be acquired if the ball is stroked sharply and firmly with the hands. Loft will be acquired if the weight is kept behind the swing and the club-face is open at impact. Better results are accomplished if players will refrain from trying to help the clubhead loft the ball. Players who have difficulty in obtaining loft should use a brassie from off the tee.

The following suggestions for executing drives from off the tee should prove helpful to you:

Planning

1. Stand on the tee and survey the fairway ahead. Consider the potential hazards. Pay particular attention to boun daries. Note the direction and velocity of the wind, if any.
2. Select a place to tee-up the ball where both feet will be on level ground at address.
3. Select and aim for a location in the fairway from which the next shot may be executed under advantageous conditions.
4. Use the driver, unless the loft, accuracy, or distance requirements are such that another club could be used to advantage.

Preparation

1. Use the overlapping grip which has been described.
2. Take a square or slightly open stance, which is about the width of the player's shoulders.
3. Play the ball from a location which is about halfway between the left foot and the center point between the feet.
4. Have the hands slightly ahead of the clubhead at address. Place the clubhead square to the line of flight. Have the center of the clubface directly behind the ball.

Execution

1. *Backswing*
   A. Take the club straight back with the *hands,* to a position which is about ear high.

1   2   3

    B. Keep the hands and wrists in their *original position* as at address, until about the halfway point in the backswing, when they begin to bend backward. Continue to bend the wrists backward gradually until they are fully cocked at the end of the backswing.

    C. Keep the left arm extended during the backswing.

    D. Simultaneously, as the hands start the backswing, bend the left knee inward and raise the left heel. Most of the weight transfers to the right leg and the hips turn to the right.

  2. *Downswing*

    A. Keep the head and shoulders *behind the swing. Pull* the hands gradually forward.

    B. Let the hands lead the clubhead. Keep the hands and wrists in the same position as at the end of the backswing, until impact, when they straighten out.

    C. Keep the arms in close to the body.

    D. As the hands approach the ball, return the left heel

7   8   9

| 4 | 5 | 6 |

LONG IRONS

Fig. 1.   A comfortable stance with the hands slightly ahead of the clubhead.

Fig. 2.   The hands take the club straight back **smartly.**

Fig. 3.   The left knee bends inward, and the left heel raises.

Fig. 4.   The wrists begin to bend backward. The hips turn to the right.

Fig. 5.   The hands and arms continue to take the club back. The wrists continue to bend backward.

Fig. 6.   The left arm is extended.

Fig. 7.   The arms and hands pull the club forward, gradually. The left heel returns to the ground, and the right knee bends inward.

Fig. 8.   The hands lead the clubhead.

Fig. 9.   The wrists straighten out.

Fig. 10.   The hands continue to move fast and outwardly. The hips turn to the left.

Fig. 11.   The head stays down until near the finish, when it turns slowly to the left from underneath.

Fig. 12.   The head and body have turned around to face the line of flight. The arms and wrists are relaxed. Most of the weight has shifted to the left leg. The right leg is relaxed, with the knee bent forward and the heel upright.

| 10 | 11 | 12 |

to the ground and kick the right knee inward. Most of the weight transfers to the left leg and the hips turn to the left.

3. *Impact*

    A. Stroke the ball sharply and firmly with the *hands*.

    B. Keep the hands moving fast and the left arm extended.

    C. Keep the head down and look at the ball.

4. *Follow through*

    A. Keep the hands moving fast and outwardly.

    B. Keep the wrists in their straightened-out position until near the finish, when they bend forward.

    C. The hips turn to the left.

    D. Keep the head in its same original position until near the finish when it turns slowly to the left from underneath.

Finish

1. The head has turned to face the line of flight, in order to follow the flight of the ball.
2. The body has turned around to face the line of flight.
3. Most of the weight has shifted to the left leg. It is supported by the heel and outside portion of the ball of the left foot.
4. The right knee is bent forward with the heel upright.
5. The hands are opposite to and slightly above the left shoulder. The arms and wrists are relaxed.
6. The clubshaft is behind the head, parallel to the shoulders and with the ground. The toe of the club is pointing towards the ground.

General

When driving from off the tee, players should concentrate upon proper alignment and the execution of a smooth stroke instead of attempting to "murder" the ball.

Summary

The following is a summary of the method of executing drives from off the tee:

PLANNING

1. Stand on the tee and survey the fairway. Observe the hazards, boundaries, and slope of the fairway. Determine the direction and velocity of the wind, if any.

2. Select a good spot in the fairway to aim for.

3. Find a level place to stand. Use the driver unless another club can be used advantageously.

PREPARATION

1. Use the overlapping grip which has been described.

2. Take a *square* stance, of about shoulder width, which is natural and comfortable.

3. Play the ball from about halfway between the left foot and the center point between the feet.

4. Have the hands slightly ahead of the clubhead at address. Place the clubhead *square* to the line of flight. Have the center of the clubface directly behind the ball.

EXECUTION

1. Take the club back smartly with the hands, to a position which is about ear high.

2. Keep the left arm extended. Keep the hands and wrists in their *same position* as at address, until about the halfway point in backswing, when the wrists begin to bend backward.

3. Simultaneously, as the hands start the backswing, bend the left knee inward and raise the left heel. Most of the weight transfers to the right leg and the hips turn to the right.

4. Keep the head behind the swing. Pull the hands gradually forward. Let the hands lead the clubhead.

5. Keep the wrists in their *same position* until impact, when they *straighten out*. The wrists stay straight until near the finish, when they begin to bend forward.

6. Keep the arms in close to the body.

7. As the hands approach the ball, return the left heel to the ground and kick the right knee inward. Most of the weight transfers to the left leg and the hips turn to the left.

1   2   3

7   8   9

13   14   15

4	5	6

10	11	12

16

WOOD SHOTS

Fig. 1—A comfortable stance with the hands slightly ahead of the clubhead. Figs. 2 and 3—The hands take the club straight back smartly. Fig. 4—The left knee bends inward and the left heel raises. Fig. 5—The wrists begin to bend backward. The hips turn to the right. Fig. 6—The hands and arms continue to take the club back, and the wrists continue to bend backward. Fig. 7—The left arm is extended. Fig. 8—The arms and hands pull the club forward, gradually. Figs. 9 and 10—The left heel returns to the ground and the right knee bends inward. Fig. 11—The hands lead the clubhead. Fig. 12—The wrists straighten out. Fig. 13—The weight stays behind the swing. The hands continue to move fast and outwardly. Fig 14—The hips turn to the left. Fig. 15—The head stays down until near the finish, when it turns slowly to the left from underneath. Fig. 16—The head and body have turned around to face the line of flight. The arms and wrists are relaxed. Most of the weight has shifted to the left leg. The right leg is relaxed with the knee bent forward and the heel upright.

8. Stroke the ball *sharply and firmly* with the hands. Keep the hands moving fast. The wrists and left arm remain straight until near the finish, when they relax.

9. Keep the head down until near the finish, when it turns slowly to the left from underneath.

FINISH

1. The head and body have turned to face the line of flight.

2. Most of the weight has shifted to the left leg and is supported by the heel and outside of the ball of the left foot. The right knee is bent forward with the heel upright.

3. The hands are opposite to and slightly above the left shoulder. The arms and wrists are relaxed.

4. The clubshaft is behind the head, parallel to the shoulders and with the ground. The toe of the club is pointing towards the ground.

BRASSIE

The method of executing Brassie shots is the same as for the

drive, with the following modifications:

1. The shot is planned while standing behind the ball, after surveying the intended line of flight.
2. The ball is played from a location which is nearer to the center point between the feet.
3. The width of the stance is slightly decreased.

Avoid the tendency to *help* the clubhead loft the ball.

SPOON

Spoon shots are similar to brassie shots with the following modifications:

1. Stand closer to the ball.
2. The ball is played from a location which is nearer to the center point between the feet.
3. The width of the stance is decreased.

NO. 4 WOOD

The stance and location of the ball for shots with a No. 4

10

FOOT AND LEG ACTION — WOOD SHOTS

Fig. 1. The weight is evenly balanced at address.

Fig. 2. The left knee bends inward and the left heel raises as the hands start the backswing.

Figs. 3 and 4. The left knee continues to bend inward and the heel continues to raise as the backswing progresses.

Fig. 5. Most of the weight has transferred to the right leg. Only the sole of the shoe underneath the big toe and the inside ball of the left foot touches the ground at the end of the backswing.

Figs. 6 and 7. The left heel returns to the ground and the right knee bends inward as the hands approach the ball.

Fig. 8. The left heel is on the ground, and the right heel has started to raise at impact.

Fig. 9. The hips turn to the left, and the right heel continues to raise.

Fig. 10. Most of the weight has transferred to the left leg. The right leg has relaxed, with the knee bent forward and the heel upright.

wood are comparable with those for long iron shots. Because No. 4 wood shots have considerable loft and a limited amount of roll, the player should aim directly at the green or other objective.

GENERAL COMMENT

Because of the variation in height and in the length of arms of the individual players, the specific distance away from the ball which players stand has not been specified. But a good general guide to follow is to have the hands fairly close to the body after the clubhead has been placed behind the ball in its natural position.

The player should not stand so far away from the ball that it becomes necessary to *reach* for the ball.

7. EXECUTING SPECIAL SHOTS

HERE are a few brief comments that might be helpful in the execution of shots involving additional factors and abnormal conditions. Special shots must be executed when the ball lies in the rough or in a trap, when the wind is strong, or the course is wet, or when the ball rests on the side of a hill.

HAZARDS IN GENERAL

It is not so much the physical difficulty involved in playing water hazards, bunkers, traps, trees, narrow boundaries, and the other hazards, as it is the player's mental attitude towards them. The average player becomes tense and tightens up when faced with the necessity of negotiating a hazard. If the player will retain a normal mental attitude and direct all of his attention to the planning and the execution of the shot, he will negotiate a majority of the hazards successfully.

Of course, it is unreasonable to expect to avoid all of the hazards all of the time. It is intended that hazards should cause the player some difficulties, but those difficulties can be minimized by retaining a normal attitude and executing a normal swing when attempting to negotiate them. Because of the variation in types of hazards, we can point out only a few good habits to practice.

1. Retain a normal mental attitude. Exercise good judgment in determining the type of shot to execute and in selecting a club with which to execute it. A club with a considerable amount of loft usually is preferable, in most cases.

2. Execute the same swing which would be executed

85

1   2   3

under normal conditions with the club that is used.

3. Stroke the ball "sharply and firmly" without any attempt to help the clubhead loft the ball.

As a general rule, such shots are just ordinary golf shots which are played under *different conditions.* A change of *conditions* does not warrant a change in the *method of execution,* unless the conditions are such that they prevent normal execution.

IN THE ROUGH

Ordinarily, it is a good policy to use an iron club when the ball is in the rough. The clubhead is sharp and will cut through the heavy grass and other vegetation better than a wood club. The use of a club with a considerable amount of loft increases the possibility of getting the ball out of heavy rough. The increased loft of the clubface decreases the amount of resistance encountered by the clubhead. *Be sure to get the ball out on the first attempt, even though it necessitates making a sacrifice of distance.*

7   8   9

4   5   6

When the club has been selected, use the same swing with it which would normally be used, after making the following modifications:

1. Take a firmer grip in order to prevent the clubhead from turning as a result of the resistance encountered.
2. Take a narrow stance in order to produce an upright swing, which permits swinging down on the ball.

The main objective is to get the ball out of the rough on the *first* attempt. The players who do that consistently will improve their average score. When a ball goes into the rough, it is intended that the player should be penalized to the extent of having to execute a shot therefrom under adverse conditions.

The player should accept the self-inflicted penalty gracefully and make the best of it by executing the type of shot which is most likely to succeed, instead of one with the odds against successful execution. If he gambles by taking long chances from the rough, he usually suffers the loss of several strokes. A wood club should not be used in the rough unless the grass is short and the "lie" of the ball is good.

10

IN THE ROUGH

Fig. 1. A narrow stance with the hands slightly ahead of the club-head. A firm grip is maintained.

Fig. 2. The hands take the club back, smartly. The left knee bends inward and the left heel raises.

Fig. 3. The arc of the backswing is a little more upright than in most of the other shots.

Fig. 4. The wrists begin to bend backward. The arms and hands continue to take the club back.

Fig. 5. The left arm is extended.

Fig. 6. The arms and hands pull the club forward. The hands lead the clubhead. The left heel returns to the ground and the right knee bends inward.

Fig. 7. The wrists straighten out.

Fig. 8. The hands continue to move fast and outwardly.

Fig. 9. The hips turn to the left. The head stays down until near the finish, when it turns slowly to the left from underneath.

Fig. 10. The head and body have turned around to face the line of flight. The arms and wrists are relaxed. The right leg has relaxed with the knee bent forward and the heel raised.

TRAP SHOTS

Because of the variation in traps and the conditions under which the shots therefrom are executed, it is well to classify trap shots accordingly. Suggested methods of executing some of the more common trap shots under given conditions are:

1. *A hard, smooth, shallow trap with smooth terrain between the trap and the green.* Use a putter or a club without much loft, and roll the ball out. Stroke the ball a little harder than when it is stroked for making a long approach putt.

2. *A hard shallow trap or wet sand with a good lie of the ball.*

   A. With medium loft requirements: Chip the ball out with a mashie or a similar club. Make a slight allowance for the resistance caused by taking a little sand or dirt. Play the ball from a location which is slightly to the right of the center point between the feet. Execute the normal stroke for chip shots, and stroke the ball a little harder.

BLAST SHOTS

Fig. 1. A firm footing has been obtained by wiggling the feet sidewise in the sand. The clubhead is above the ball at address in order to comply with the rule against soleing the clubhead in sand traps.
Fig. 2. The hands take the club back. The left knee bends inward and the left heel raises. The hips turn to the right.
Fig. 3. The wrists begin to bend backward.
Fig. 4. The left arm is fully extended.
Fig. 5. The arms and hands pull the club forward, gradually. The hands lead the clubhead. The left heel returns to the ground and the right knee bends inward.
Fig. 6. The wrists straighten out. The clubhead strikes the sand an inch or two **behind** the ball.
Figs. 7 and 8. The hands continue to move towards the hole. The hips turn to the left.
Fig. 9. The arms, hands, and clubshaft are extended forward. The wrists are in a straightened-out position. Most of the weight has been transferred to the left leg. The right knee is bent forward slightly, and the right heel is slightly raised.

1   2   3

4   5   6

7   8   9

    B. With considerable loft requirements: Chip the ball
       out with a lofted club in the same manner as de-
       scribed above.
3. *A deep trap with soft dry sand.* Blast the ball out with a
sand wedge or niblick.
The method of execution is broken down as follows:
    A. Preparation.
      1. Use the normal overlapping grip.
      2. Play the ball from about the center point between
         the feet.
      3. Take a comfortable stance of medium width.
         Wiggle the feet sidewise in the sand to obtain a
         firm footing.
      4. Place the hands ahead of the clubhead at address.
    B. Execution.
      1. Take the hands back to a position which is about
         shoulder high.
      2. *Keep the head down. Stay behind the swing.*
      3. Hit an inch or two back of the ball. Take sand in
         proportion to the lie of the ball and the texture of
         the sand.
      4. Execute the stroke in a normal manner, without
         attempting to add force or trying to help the club-
         head loft the ball.
    C. Finish.

    At the finish, the arms, hands, and clubshaft are ex-
tended well forward, in the direction of the hole. The
hands are about waist high. The head has turned to face
the hole.

    It is extremely difficult and very hazardous to blast out
of wet sand or sand which is coarse and heavy. The use
of a chip shot or a modified pitch shot is safer out of wet
or heavy sand when conditions permit their use.

4. *Shots from a bunker or trap, which require distance and
loft:*
    A. Use a club with sufficient loft to raise the ball above

the lip of the trap. *Sacrifice distance for loft*, if any doubt exists.

B. Execute a normal stroke with the club that is used, if conditions permit.

Be sure to get out of the trap or bunker on the *first attempt*. Practice at getting out of traps is a means of saving strokes.

IN THE WOODS OR AMONG TREES

Attempt to find an opening through which to execute a lofted shot. If that is impossible, select an opening underneath the branches through which to execute a low shot and use a club without much loft. Use about one-half or three-quarters of a full swing in executing the stroke.

Be sure to get the ball into a location from which to execute the next shot under favorable conditions. Gambling against unfavorable odds usually results in the loss of strokes.

PLAYING THE WIND

The degree to which the wind affects the flight of a golf ball is determined by the velocity of the wind and the type of shot which is executed. A strong wind is likely to have more effect upon a shot in which the ball is lofted high into the air.

The wind does affect the flight of a ball and has to be considered in planning and executing a shot. But as a general rule, it has a greater mental effect upon the player than it does upon the flight of the ball.

Here are some pointers which might be helpful when playing in the wind:

1. *When playing against the wind.*

   A. Use a stronger club than would be used under normal conditions. Reduce the length of the swing if necessary.

   B. Keep the flight of the ball low when possible. Make adequate allowance for roll.

   C. Aim directly at the objective or beyond it on shots which have much loft. Make limited allowance for roll, if any. The ball does not roll much after landing, when lofted shots are executed against the wind.

2. *When playing with the wind.*
   A. Use a weaker club than would ordinarily be used for the same shot under normal conditions.
   B. Aim short of the objective. Make adequate allowance for roll. The ball rolls freely when the wind blows in the same direction as the flight of the ball.
3. *When playing in a cross wind.*
   Aim to the right or left of the desired objective, in proportion to the velocity of the wind and its likely effect upon that particular type of shot.

PLAYING ON A WET COURSE

When the course is wet and heavy, the player should attempt to execute the type of shots which will best conform with the conditions that exist.

The following pointers may help your play on a wet course:

1. Select a club with considerable loft with which to execute the shots. The ball rolls very little, if any, after landing.
2. Get a firm footing in order to prevent the feet from slipping while executing a shot.
3. Because of the limited roll of the ball after landing, aim directly at the objective or approximately thereto. The ball usually stops very close to where it lands on wet greens.
4. Chip or pitch the ball out of traps around the greens. The execution of a blast shot from wet sand or mud is so hazardous that it is wise to avoid attempting it when possible.
5. Some players use a club with a little loft on the face to make approach putts if the green is extremely wet or if there is water between the ball and the cup. The possibility of damage to the green makes this undesirable, except in important matches.

When playing in the rain, it is well to dry off the grip of the club with a towel or cloth just before executing a shot. It will enable the maintenance of a good grip throughout the stroke.

UPHILL LIE

Some of the important points to remember in playing shots from an uphill lie are presented herewith:

1. It is not necessary to use a club with much loft because the clubhead gets well underneath the ball.
2. Attempt to maintain good balance. Avoid trying to hold onto the ground with the feet.
3. The ball is played from about the same location which it would normally be played from, or slightly forward therefrom, depending upon the amount of slope.
4. On long shots, aim slightly to the right of the objective, because the ball is most likely to hook.
5. Short shots are played in the normal way.

Some players bend their left knee slightly forward at address in order to keep the weight equalized on both feet.

DOWNHILL LIE

When playing shots from a downhill lie, remember these pointers:

1. Use a club with a considerable amount of loft because it is difficult for the clubhead to get underneath the ball.
2. Attempt to maintain a good balance. Avoid trying to hold onto the ground with the feet. Take a slightly open stance.
3. From a slight slope, play the ball from a location which is about halfway between the right foot and the center point between the feet. Have the ball nearer to the right foot as the slope becomes steeper.
4. On long shots, aim slightly to the left of the objective, because the ball is most likely to slice.
5. The arc of the swing is upright, which permits swinging down on the ball.
6. Stroke the ball in a normal manner, without any attempt to *scoop the ball or help the club*.
7. Execute short shots in the normal way.

Some players bend their right knee slightly forward in

order to equalize the weight on both of the feet.

SIDEHILL LIE

When playing sidehill lies, it is well to observe the following points:

1. Attempt to maintain good balance. Avoid trying to hold onto the ground with the feet.
2. Use a shorter club when the slope of the hill is toward the player. Stand closer to the ball, because of a tendency to fall away from the ball. If the player is standing on level ground, the same stance is used which would be used under normal conditions.
3. Use a longer club when the slope of the hill is away from the player. Stand farther away from the ball, because of a tendency to fall toward the ball. If the player is standing on level ground, the same stance is employed as under normal conditions.

The player must exercise his own judgment to determine the type of stance to take if the hill slopes in more than one direction.

Players should practice executing shots which involve additional factors and abnormal conditions so that they can execute them with a reasonable degree of skill when playing.

8. REASONS FOR INCORRECT SHOTS

PLAYERS of all classes experience a few shots which are hit incorrectly. Players of the average class experience them more frequently and to a higher degree than players who are more highly skilled. There are two reasons for this. First, because the more highly skilled players usually have a reasonably correct swing; it does not get out of order as easily or as often as the swing of the less skillful players. Second, because the more skillful players are able to analyze their swing, detect the probable cause of the incorrectly hit shot and soon correct it; whereas the less skillful players, being unable to do so, usually continue to hit shots incorrectly until someone helps them to get straightened out.

Let us discuss the nature and causes of shots which are incorrectly hit.

HOOKS, SLICES, SMOTHERED SHOTS, AND SHANKED SHOTS

When a player has difficulty consistently because of hooks, slices, smothered shots, or shanked shots, usually the trouble is due to a fundamental weakness in his swing. *The necessary correction of fundamentals should be made only upon the advice of a competent professional.* However, there are many instances where the player's swing is fundamentally sound, but where he has difficulty occasionally because of poor timing, or because of the necessity of some slight adjustment in his swing.

For the benefit of those who have trouble only occasionally, some of the more common causes of these difficulties are dealt with here:

95

Hooks

1. Use of a grip which partially closes the clubface.
2. Use of a closed stance at address.
3. Playing the ball from a location which is back towards the right foot.
4. Overpowering of the left hand by the right hand, thus dominating the stroke.
5. Turning the body too much in the downswing.

Slices

1. Use of a grip which leaves the clubface at impact open too much, or at an improper angle.
2. Use of too open a stance.
3. Lack of proper foot and knee action in the swing.
4. Turning the body in the early stages of the downswing, which causes the arc of the swing to be from the outside in. (This is commonly referred to as "cutting across the ball.")
5. Having the body ahead of the hands in the downswing.
6. A tendency at impact to quit or lessen the speed of the clubhead.
7. Playing the ball from too far forward a position.

Smothered Shots

1. Use of a grip which leaves the clubface closed too much at impact.
2. Permitting the right hand to lift the club or to take it too far inside during the backswing.
3. Poor wrist action which closes the clubface too much.
4. Having the body ahead of the hands in the downswing. (Usually this results from a "forward lunge" at the start of the downswing, because of an effort to add force to the stroke.)

Shanked Shots

1. Gripping the club too tightly.
2. Bending the left arm during the backswing.
3. Turning the shoulders or hips at the start of the down swing.
4. Failure to keep the head and body behind the stroke

during the downswing. (This is a very common mistake.)

5. Failure to keep the left arm close to the body in the downswing.

6. Attempting to guide or steer the ball at impact, instead of swinging the hands freely.

Hitting the Ground

Hitting the ground behind the ball usually results from one or more of the following causes:

1. Standing too close to the ball at address.

2. Failure to keep the right leg firm during the backswing.

3. Dipping the head and upper part of body at the start of the downswing.

4. Throwing the clubhead at the start of the downswing.

5. Dropping the right shoulder during the downswing.

6. Looking up before impact with the ball.

In some instances the difficulty may be due to a combination of factors. Players who have difficulties of this nature should check each possible reason at the practice tee. Usually the difficulty can be determined and corrected by the process of elimination.

9. CONCLUSION

THIS book has been written in such a manner that it provides about all the information which an average golfer needs to know. The importance of learning and mastering the mechanics of a swing which are fundamentally sound and well-timed has been stressed. The mechanics of the swing and the manner of co-ordinating them into a smooth and well-timed swing have been described. The method of planning and executing the various types of shots has been stated in detail and in summary form. The essentials have been included, the nonessentials have been omitted. The authors have provided scientific methods and sound fundamentals which will improve the average golfer's game, if properly applied. Putting them into practice requires some effort on the part of players.

Changes made in the mechanics or in the method of applying the mechanics to the swing usually affect the player's score adversely until such changes have become habitual. It is unreasonable to expect the player to score well when his attention is concentrated upon mechanics or methods. To make a low score requires that the player's attention be concentrated upon the planning and execution of each shot.

Changes in the swing should be made during practice or at such times when the player is not attempting to make a low score. Attempts to make changes during actual play usually results in confusion and a loss of confidence. It is suggested that players consider the merits of potential changes carefully before attempting to adopt them. It is well to consult a competent professional instructor as to the merits of the proposed changes and to make such changes under his guidance.

But after you decide to make changes, give the new method a chance to produce satisfactory results. It takes time to accomplish a reasonable degree of consistent performance without the necessity of having to consciously direct one's efforts. There is no magic button to push which will make the change to perfection. It takes time and effort. Be *realistic* about it, like Mr. B. A. Success. Do not be like Mr. I. Hope.

If Mr. B. A. Success were psychoanalyzed in order to determine why he was successful at golf, we should probably find these characteristics in his play:

1. He is enthusiastic about golf and has developed a good attitude towards it.

2. He has made a scientific approach to the game in order to determine the correct methods and mechanics.

3. He is realistic and not disposed towards "kidding" himself. Frequently, he consults the club professional or a competent instructor in order to be sure that he makes the proper application of the correct methods.

4. He is sufficiently energetic to practice and to master the mechanics of golf.

5. His mastery of the mechanics permits him to relax and to concentrate on the planning and the execution of each shot.

6. His keen understanding of the game enables him to exercise good judgment in selecting the type of shot to execute under existing conditions.

7. His skill creates a high degree of confidence; he really enjoys the game.

It might be well for Mr. Average Golfer to adopt Mr. B. A. Success as his ideal and to follow in his footsteps.

Come on, fellows. Let's quit being permanent residents of the "Bear Country." Let's find out what the fairways look like. Let's make the fairways safe. Let's quit digging those divots "of atomic-bomb-crater proportions" for other golfers to fall into. Let's apply the basic principles of good golf described in this book and get a real thrill out of improving our game.

APPENDIX

APPENDIX A

GOLF CLUBS AND THEIR USES

THE skill of a workman is largely dependent upon the type of tools he uses. Likewise, the skill of a golfer is largely dependent upon the type of clubs he uses. It is essential that the clubs be of good quality. A certain number of clubs are essential.

A substantial number of clubs should be used to provide for a higher degree of refinement, and at the same time simplification of play. Naturally, a greater number of clubs increases the flexibility which permits and encourages a higher degree of refinement in play. An adequate number of clubs simplifies play in providing a club for each type of shot without requiring players to change their swing in order to execute the various types of shots.

There is some variation in the method of numbering clubs, but they are fairly well standardized among the leading club manufacturers. In order to familiarize players with the various clubs and their uses, a list of standard clubs and commonly used special clubs is given here.

Wood Clubs

NO.	NAME	DESCRIPTION	COMMON USE
1	Driver	A long shaft with a straight face (not much pitch or loft on the clubface.)	Used to drive from the tee with the ball teed up.
2	Brassie	A long shaft with a slightly pitched clubface.	Used to execute long shots from the fairway. Frequently used from the tee where the loft or distance requirements make it preferable to the driver.
3	Spoon	A medium-long shaft with a pitched clubface.	Used to execute long shots from the fairway which require loft or where the lie of the ball is not good. Frequently used from the tee on long par 3 holes.

103

NO. NAME	DESCRIPTION	COMMON USE
4 Lofted Spoon	A medium-long shaft with a highly pitched clubface.	Used to execute long shots from the fairway which require a high degree of loft or where the lie of the ball is unusually bad. Frequently used from the tee on par 3 holes.
5 Baffie	A short shaft with a very highly pitched clubface.	Used instead of number 3 or 4 iron by players who prefer to use wood clubs instead of iron clubs. *It is a special club which is not commonly used.*

Iron Clubs

1 Driving Iron	A long shaft with a very straight club-face. (V e r y little pitch or loft on the clubface.)	Used from the tee with the ball teed up on long par 3 holes. Sometimes used from the fairway against the wind where the lie of the ball is good.
2 Midiron	A long shaft with a fairly straight club-face. (The club provides more loft than the pitch of the club-face indicates.)	Used from the fairway on long iron shots. Frequently used from the tee on par 3 holes of medium length, with or without the ball being teed up.
3 Midiron of medium loft.	A long shaft with a slightly pitched club-face. (The club provides a considerable amount of loft.)	Used from the fairway on long iron shots which require loft and a considerable amount of distance. Frequently used from the tee on par 3 holes of medium distance, with or without the ball being teed up.
4 Midiron of considerable loft.	A medium-long shaft with a fair degree of pitch on the club-face. A combination club which provides loft and distance.	Used from the fairway on iron shots of medium distance. Frequently used from the tee on par 3 holes which are within its distance range. Ample loft of the clubface does not require that the ball be teed up.
5 Mashie	A shaft of medium length with a pitched clubface. Provides a reasonable amount of distance with considerable loft.	Used from the fairway on shots which do not require a considerable amount of distance. The loft of clubface renders it valuable in clearing hazards. Commonly used for chip shots and from the tee on the shorter par 3 holes.

NO. NAME	DESCRIPTION	COMMON USE
6 Spade-Mashie	A shorter shaft than the mashie with a higher d e g r e e of pitch on the clubface.	Used from the fairway on shots of limited distance requirements. The loft of clubface provides a considerable amount of loft. Used for chip shots and short pitch shots which permit a considerable amount of roll after the ball lands on the green. Used from the tee on short par 3 holes.
7 Mashie-Niblick	A short shaft with a high degree of pitch o n t h e clubface, which provides a certain amount of backspin.	Used from the fairway on shots which require a considerable amount of loft but very little distance. Commonly used for pitch shots, short approach shots to the green, to clear hazards, in the rough, or in traps. A good all-round club for shots which do not require distance. Sometimes used from the tee on very short par 3 holes.
8 Lofted Mashie-Niblick	A short shaft with a very high degree of pitch on the clubface.	Used for pitch shots to the green which require that the ball stops soon after it lands. Used for all types of short shots which require loft. Frequently used in traps and in the rough.
9 Niblick	A short shaft with an extremely high degree of pitch on the clubface.	Used for pitch shots to the green which require that the ball stop suddenly after it lands. Used for all types of shots which require a high degree of loft. A good club to use in traps and in the rough. In the absence of a sand wedge, it is commonly used to execute blast shots from traps which have soft, dry sand.
10 Putter	A very short shaft with straight face. (No pitch or loft.)	Used on the green to putt with. Sometimes used to roll the ball on to the green from near the edge or out of hard, shallow traps where the terrain between the ball and the green is smooth.

Special Clubs

Chip-Iron	A very short shaft with a slight amount of pitch on the clubface.	Used near the edge of the green to chip the ball onto the green.

NAME	DESCRIPTION	COMMON USE
Pitching-Iron	A weighted club with a short shaft and a high degree of pitch on the clubface.	Used to pitch the ball onto the green and for other lofted shots.
Sand-Wedge	A weighted club with a short shaft and an extremely high degree of pitch on the clubface	Used to execute blast shots from traps which have soft, dry sand. Sometimes used to execute pitch shots which require that the ball stop suddenly after it lands. Use of the sand-wedge for pitch shots requires a good lie of the ball and practice with it.

There are other clubs manufactured, but their deviation from the standard clubs is too slight to warrant an attempt to list all of them.

For tournament play, a maximum of fourteen clubs has been established, but a minimum of five clubs is necessary in order to play with a passable degree of refinement. Tournament players should carry near the maximum number of clubs, but it is not necessary for the average golfer.

As a guide, it is well to start out with a small number of clubs and to increase their number as the player acquires sufficient skill to effect a higher degree of refinement in play. It is easier to become well acquainted with a few clubs before additions are made.

A suggested list of clubs to begin playing with is as follows:

	NUMBER	NAME
Wood Clubs	2	Brassie
Iron Clubs	2	Midiron
	5	Mashie
	7	Mashie-Niblick
	10 or 9	Putter

The order of additions is dependent upon the skill of individual players and the type of courses which are played. A suggested order of additions, which will apply to a substantial majority of players, is as follows.

	NUMBER	NAME
Wood Clubs	3	Spoon
	1	Driver
	4	Lofted-Spoon
Iron Clubs	4	Lofted Midiron
	8 or 9	Lofted Mashie-Niblick or Niblick
	6	Spade-Mashie
	3	Midiron of Medium loft
	1	Driving Iron
Special Clubs		Sand Wedge
		Chip Iron
		Pitching Iron

Men players should purchase clubs for men that are of average length and weight and which have good balance. Women players should purchase clubs for women that are of average length and weight and which have good balance. Above all, clubs should "feel" good to the player who intends to use them.

APPENDIX B

HOW TO PLAY WITH GOOD PLAYERS

THERE seems to be a feeling on the part of beginners and golfers who do not make low scores that the better golfers dislike to play with them because they do not play equally as well. As a general rule, that is not the case. However, the better golfers do like to play with other good players most of the time because stiff competition stimulates an added interest in the game.

It is safe to say that the better golfers really enjoy an occasional round with golfers who do not score as well as they do. Particularly so, if the individuals are good sports and observe the rules of etiquette. It provides an opportunity for the better players to experiment with some new stance or grip which they have wanted to try but would not do so when playing with other good golfers because the stiff competition prohibited it.

Occasionally, good players like to play a game which does not require the concentration and effort necessary to make a low score. They just want to relax and enjoy the fresh air and companionship of other golfers. The absence of stiff competition encourages the observation of scenery, sociable conversation, and a carefree attitude which rarely exists when they are under the pressure of stiff competition.

The good players do not like to deviate from their established practice of playing frequently with golfers of equal skill, but most of them do enjoy an occasional round with a player of less skill who makes a desirable companion. If they like him, they will be tolerant of his lack of skill at golf. As a matter of fact, the majority of them are more tolerant than players who have not developed a high degree of skill.

It is safe to say that most of them display a helpful attitude. They are willing to help the less skillful players by giving them valuable pointers on the fine points of the game to the extent that it does not detract from their own game. The display of a helpful attitude up to a certain point does not mean that they are willing to teach one the fundamentals of the game. That is a job for the professional instructor, but most of the good players are willing to help golfers who really try to learn.

The average golfer should make it a point to play an occasional game with some good player. "Well, Mr. Author," you might ask, "that is an excellent suggestion, but how do I go about it?" To which Mr. Author replies, "That is a good $64 question," and after severely straining his mental capacity, comes up with the following suggestions:

1. Select some good golfer who is a neighbor, club member, or an acquaintance with whom you share a common interest.

2. Explain that you would like to play with him sometime when he does not have plans to play with other good players. Within all probability, he will suggest a possible time when it might be convenient for him to play with you or he will arrange to contact you when an opportune occasion arises. He will be glad to know of someone who wants to play with him in the event that he does not have plans or on an occasion when it is necessary for him to change his plans upon short notice.

3. Be a good sport and observe the rules of etiquette. Display a sense of humor if you make a bad shot or encounter abnormal difficulties. Expect some difficulties and accept them gracefully. Avoid making alibis, becoming angry, or getting panicky. Be such a pleasant companion that your partner will want to play with you again.

4. Acknowledge your lack of skill and show a desire to learn. Ask an occasional question about some fundamental or fine point of the game, but do not detract from your companion's game. Listen attentively to his answer or anything which he tells you.

5. Show your appreciation that he played with you. Acknowledge and praise his efforts to help you.

Golfers should create opportunities to play with good players. It has a good psychological effect. A few rounds with good players will make the average golfer raise his sights and create a desire to improve. Seeing others play well makes him realize that it can be done, if the correct methods are properly applied. He becomes possessed with the desire to learn how to make the proper application of correct methods. *The golf bug has bitten him.* The game has another "dyed-in-the-wool" enthusiast. He consults a professional instructor. He begins to improve. Before long he is a respectable week-end golfer. The new interest in life has changed his personality. He wonders why he didn't take up golf sooner.

Once the golf bug bites you, it gets into your blood. There is something about it that causes players to continuously seek to improve. No matter how well one plays he still tries to improve. Golfers often threaten to quit the game and to throw their clubs away when they fail to play well, but the junk yards have not had to increase their size in order to make room for the golf clubs which "ex-golfers" have thrown away.

The game provides many thrills, a lot of healthful recreation, good companionship, and some disappointments. The world seems bright when one plays well and seems dark when one plays poorly. Usually, the periods when it looks dark are of short duration. Eventually, one regains his touch and begins to hit the ball.

Any game which is so simple that it does not require the best efforts of the participants and which fails to provide some uncertainties usually lacks interest. The uncertainties of golf make it a game of unusual interest. The chance of looking at the world through rose-colored glasses most of the time and seeing it through dark glasses some of the time is the novelty which makes it so interesting. But who expects to look at the world or anything else through a pair of rose-colored glasses all of the time. That would make life uninteresting, and besides, it is bad for the eyes.

APPENDIX C

GOLF ETIQUETTE

I N THE final analysis, the etiquette of golf consists in being courteous, considerate of others, and in the display of good manners. It is no different from the etiquette of the social and business world. Both are based upon courtesy and common sense. In order to familiarize players with the etiquette of golf, a list of the standard rules of etiquette are given below. The rules are presented with permission of the United States Golf Association.

1. No one should move or talk or stand close to or directly behind the ball or the hole when a player is making a stroke.
2. The player who has the "honour" should be allowed to play before his opponent tees his ball.
3. No player should play until the party in front is out of range.
4. When the result of a hole has been determined, players should immediately leave the putting green.
5. Players, while looking for a lost ball, should allow other matches coming up to pass them; they should signal to the players following them to pass; and having given such a signal, they should not continue their play until these players have passed and are out of range.
6. A player should see that any turf cut or displaced by him is at once replaced and pressed down.
7. Players should carefully fill up all holes made in a bunker.
8. Players should see that their caddies do not injure the holes by standing close to them when the ground is soft, or in replacing the flag-stick.

9. A player who has incurred a penalty should intimate the fact to his opponent as soon as possible.

10. Players should at all times play without undue delay.

Many golf clubs print the local rules which govern play and special rules of etiquette which are to be observed on the back of their score cards. It is suggested that players refer to the back of their score cards before playing a strange course.

It is generally conceded that the better players observe the rules of etiquette more carefully than the inexperienced players. The possible reason for this is that the good player's high degree of skill gives him a feeling of security which the less-skillful player lacks. The good player maintains a cool, calm, and collected attitude under adverse conditions, whereas the less-skillful player is more likely to become panicky when something goes wrong.

Most golfers will tolerate and excuse a lack of skill but are intolerant of breaches of etiquette. They see no reason to excuse a lack of good manners. It is distracting to have someone move or talk while a player is executing a shot. It is annoying to be distracted or delayed unnecessarily during play.

One rarely chooses associates in the social or business world who lack courtesy and good manners. Likewise golfers rarely choose companions who lack these qualities. If golfers expect to make desirable companions, they must observe the rules of etiquette.

APPENDIX D

GLOSSARY OF TERMS USED IN GOLF

Ace. A hole scored in one stroke.

Addressing the Ball. Putting one's self in a position to hit the ball.

All square. Term used to express that the score stands even.

Approaching. Playing a ball onto the putting green.

Away. The player whose ball lies farthest away from the hole is said to be away.

Back spin. Rotating of the ball imparted by striking the ball a descending blow, similar to a draw shot in billiards.

Ball lost. A ball is "lost" if it be not found within five minutes after the player's side or his or their caddies have begun to search for it, and if subsequently found may not be played.

Birdie. A hole scored in one stroke less than par.

Bogey. A hole scored in one stroke over par.

Bunker. A trap or pit hazard with or without sand.

Bye. The holes remaining after one side has become more "holes up" than the total holes remaining to be played.

Caddie. A person who carries the clubs.

Carry. The distance the ball travels between the striking point and the landing point.

Casual water. Any temporary accumulation of water which is not one of the ordinary and recognized hazards of the course.

Club. An implement with which the ball is struck.

Course. The "course" is the whole area within which play is permitted. More particularly, it is the ground between the holes which is specially prepared for play.

Cup. An expression used to refer to the hole.

Dead. A ball is said to be "dead" when it is so near the hole that putting it in on the next stroke is a "dead" certainty. A ball is said to "fall dead" when it lands without much run.

113

Divot. A piece of turf cut or dug out while striking the ball with the club.

Dormy. One side is said to be "dormy" when it is as many holes up as remain to be played.

Eagle. A hole scored in two strokes less than par.

Face. The surface of the club with which the ball is struck.

Fairway. The expanse of ground, extending in whole or in part from the tee to the green, especially prepared for play with the grass cut shorter than the rough.

Follow through. The continuation of the stroke after the ball has been struck.

"Fore!" A cry of warning to people in line of play.

Four-ball match. A match in which two players to a side are engaged, each playing his own ball. A four-ball match implies that each of the four players uses his own ball, and they may all play against each other or may play in pairs, the best ball of each pair scoring.

Foursome. A round of golf in which four players participate, using two or four balls.

Green. The "putting-green" is all ground, except hazards, within twenty yards of the hole.

Grip. (a) The upper part of the club-shaft which is held in the hands; (b) The method of holding the club, such as the overlapping, interlocking, and plain grip.

Half. Used to indicate that two players scored alike on a hole.

Half-shot. A shot played with a half swing.

Halved. A hole is "halved" when both sides have played it in the same number of strokes. A round is "halved" when each side has won and lost the same number of holes.

Handicap. A method used to rate or equalize players, based upon the relationship of their score to par.

Hazard. Any bunker, water (except *casual water*), ditch, sand, or road.

Hole. (a) The circular opening in the ground into which the ball is played, being $4\frac{1}{4}$ in. in diameter and 4 in. deep; (b) A unit of play including teeing ground, putting green, and all intermediate ground.

Hole-out. To make the final stroke in playing the ball into the hole.

Honour. The player or side which plays first from a teeing ground is said to have the honour.

Hook. To cause the ball to swerve to the left of its original line of flight.

Lie. The position of the ball on the ground such as a "good lie," or "a bad lie."

Like. The stroke which makes the player's score equal to his opponent's in the course of playing a hole.

Like-as-we-lie. Said when both sides have played the same number of strokes.

Line. The direction of the hole being played, from where the ball lies.

Loft. (a) Pitch or slope of the face of a club (tending to drive the ball upward); (b) To raise the ball into the air.

Long game. The strokes where distance is required.

Match-play. Play in which the score is determined by holes won and lost.

Medal-play. Play in which the score is determined by the total of strokes taken on the round.

Nassau. A method of scoring in which three points are involved—one on the first nine holes, one on the second nine, and one on the full eighteen.

Out-of-bounds. Any ground outside of the defined playing zone.

Par. Theoretically perfect play, which has been calculated on the number of strokes required to reach the green, plus two putts. Distance is the important factor in determining the par for a hole, computed on the following distances: (1) All distances up to 250 yds., par 3; (2) 251 to 445, par 4; (3) 446 to 600, par 5; (4) over 600, par 6. Each hole should be measured horizontally from the middle of the tee to the center of the green, following the planned line of play.

Penalty stroke. A "penalty stroke" is a stroke added to the score of a player or a side under certain rules, and does not affect the rotation of play.

Pitch. To loft a ball into the air.

Pitch-and-run. To play the ball so that a part of the distance is covered by the roll of the ball after it strikes the ground.

Press. An effort to hit the ball too hard or too far.

Provisional ball. If a ball has been played on to a part of the course where it is likely to be lost or unplayable, the player may, in order to save delay, at once play another ball provisionally, but if the first ball be neither lost nor unplayable it shall continue in play without penalty.

Pull. A shot that goes off line to the left.

Putt. The stroke used on the putting green.

Rough. Any ground within bounds other than the fairway—usually long grass, weeds or other vegetation.

Run. The roll of the ball after landing.

Short game. Shots where the distance requirements are less than 100 yards, usually near the green.

Single. A match between two players.

Slice. A ball which is hit incorrectly so that it curves to the right.

Sole. The bottom part of the clubhead which rests on the ground.

Square. Any point in a match where the score is even.

Stroke. A forward movement of the club made with the intention of striking the ball.

Swing. A combination of all movements involved in the execution of a golf stroke.

Tee. A little mound or peg which is used to drive the ball from the teeing ground.

Teeing-ground. The starting point for each hole.

Threesome. A round of golf in which three players participate.

Through-the-green. The whole of the course except the teeing ground, the putting green, and hazards.

Toe. The outward point of the clubhead sometimes referred to as the nose of the club.

Topped shot. To hit the ball above the center.

Up. When a player or players is ahead in the score, either in strokes or holes.

INDEX

117